Who Says
We Never Listen?
Margaret Jones
Sarah Jones-Hernandez

Hardcover: 979-8-9946956-0-9
Paperback: 979-8-9946956-1-6
ebook: 979-8-9946956-2-3

# Table of Contents

*To Our Mother- Evelyn Jones*

*We love you and we thank you for your enthusiastic and vivid stories*

## *Time and Healing*

"Behold, I make all things new..." Revelation 21:5 (KJV)

On my way to work one Wednesday afternoon, I passed a cemetery while a funeral service was in progress. Among the many sad, tear-stained faces, I glimpsed the countenance of one young woman. There was a look of paralyzed grief in her eyes as she stared at a tot-sized casket and clutched a well-loved teddy bear. After saying a prayer for the child and the family, I drove to work. But that young woman's face continued to haunt me.

Each week I saw different flowers on the child's grave; at Christmas, a tiny, decorated tree; at Easter, a basket with a chocolate bunny; and in March, a carnation birthday cake with four sparkler candles. Occasionally, I would see the woman, and I took heart, because I could see the small signs of emotional recovery.

Then, last week, I saw something that made me laugh and cry at the same time. There was the mother kneeling at the tiny graveside; but instead of horrifying grief, I saw in her face a sense of serenity and peace. She touched her fingers to her lips, and then transferred the kiss to the headstone. She stood up, took a deep breath, and smiled. So did I, for I saw the unmistakable signs of pregnancy. The dead child was not forgotten; rather, the mother had gained the strength and courage to remand her child's soul into the everlasting, ever-loving care of God.

*Evelyn Jones RN, Staff Nurse*

(First published in Staff Newsletter.
No edits were made from original publication.)

# Introduction

As a child, I dreaded those moments when my mother would become nostalgic over a letter, or a piece of jewelry, or some other knick-knack. Inevitably, she'd launch into a lengthy description of the time and place and circumstances surrounding a memory that she was relaying to me. As most pre-teens tend to do, I took my mom's stories at face value. I was sure that my mother was trying to *bore me to death*! Nevertheless, I listened to her, knowing fully that the moment she stopped talking I would snap out of the coma. Some of her favorite memories were revisited so often that I knew them by heart. She would get really mad when I finished a story she was telling before she had the chance to.

As I got older, I learned to appreciate all that she could teach me about our past. As much as I tried to deny it, I knew that my parents *were* young once — they got into trouble, fell in love, made mistakes, and explored the world with wide-eyed wonder. Through her recollections I got to know the grandfather I never met, the people she went to school with, a world without modern technology, more about the politics of the 50s and 60s, and even the string of events that brought my parents together. Until recently, I feared that, as time went by, her stories would eventually fade away. Much of our own family history was yet to be revealed and there were simply not enough hours in the day to allow for work, school, church activities, friends, *AND* interrogating my family about the past.

In the summer of 2002, my younger sister Margaret and our mother visited Margaret's college creative writing professor, Dr. Koolitz. Shortly after they arrived at the professor's home, Mom had Dr. Koolitz enraptured in a tale about the time she taught her friend how to read. When the story concluded, Dr. Koolitz turned to Margaret and said, in earnest, "You should make a story out of that." And, thus, the seed was planted.

Margaret tried to keep her ideas of starting a book to herself but, after a few weeks, she began bursting at the seams with excitement until she finally broke down and confided in me. I immediately fell in love with the idea. We decided to team up to write this tribute to our mother, and we vowed to keep it a secret from her until the book was published. However, I am grateful that we broke that vow and shared our planned endeavor with her because she passed away before this project came to fruition.

We chose to tell the stories from her point of view to preserve the relationships of the people and places in the dynamic which *we* were first introduced to them. However, some details have been added or edited for clarification purposes. It is important to emphasize that this is Mom's narrative, the way she remembered these events and recounted them to us. In the following pages, Margaret and I have attempted to capture some of our mom's favorite stories, and we hope you'll enjoy them as much as we have.

*Sarah LaDema Jones-Hernandez*

# 1910s - 1940s

# Babies Come from Tree Stumps

Some of my favorite memories stem from the visits we had with my grandma LaDema "Dema" Scott. I especially loved hearing stories about Mama's childhood. During one of our many visits, I was shocked to hear Grandma say something about Mama's adoption. When I mentioned this to Mama, she looked at me and said in her firmest voice, "*That* woman is my mother." Although I was still curious, I never asked about it again. A few years later, Mama told me the truth about her past.

Mama, Florence, was the second of three girls. Her birth father, Lawrence, was a farmer and her birth mother, Lily, stayed at home to take care of the children. Just after the birth of her third child, Lily became extremely ill. She developed a condition called puerperal fever, commonly known as childbed fever. After only a few days, Lily passed away. Her death put Lawrence in a terrible position. He knew that it would be difficult to successfully run his farm *and* raise three children; to lighten his load, he gave the girls away to be raised by family members.

In the early 1900s, there was no such thing as formal adoption. Instead, a person simply assumed responsibility for a child that needed a family. Mama's older sister, Dorothy, went to Lily's parents, my great-grandma and great-grandpa Boger. The newborn, Helena, was given to Lily's sister Lottie and her husband James. Unfortunately, four months after they took Helena in, the baby died of pneumonia. Mama was placed with Lily's other sister, Dema, and Dema's husband Lloyd. She was just 21 months old.

When Grandpa Lawrence gave Mama away, he went into his backyard and sat her on a tree stump. Then, he walked away and never looked back. Moments later, Dema and Lloyd came to claim Mama. Before picking her up, they snapped a picture of her sitting there. Now, whenever I hear someone ask where babies come from, I can still hear Mama say, "Babies come from tree stumps, and I've got the picture to prove it."

*Mama (Florence), April 1921*

# The Value of a Dollar

I always viewed my daddy, George, as a pillar of strength because he worked hard to support the family and never once complained. It was difficult for me to visualize him in any other role than the head of our family, let alone as a young boy. When I was only ten years old, he died after suffering a heart attack. After he passed away, I became hungry for stories that anyone could tell me about him because I feared that his memory would fade in my mind. Due to my persistence, I heard tales of Daddy's work, his army days, and his role in our family. Periodically, however, I had the pleasure of hearing a story about Daddy's mischievous childhood.

My grandparents, Robert and Evelyn, had seven children. Daddy had one older brother, Robert, three younger sisters, Margaret, Ruth and Helen, and two younger brothers, Frank and William. They were all very young when the United States was in The Great Depression. The country was suffering from an economic crisis and most families survived on rations provided by the government. During this time, it was an incredible luxury to eat steak or go to a movie. Money was spent only on the bare necessities. Every penny left after these expenses were paid went straight to charities to help the country out of its predicament.

My grandfather, Robert, lived by those ideals and spent his money with extreme caution. In addition to the essentials, he set aside a small amount of his income for home maintenance and repairs. When Daddy was around nine years old, Grandpa decided that it was time to weather the roof. To keep roof shingles in good condition it was common practice to paint them. He gave Daddy five dollars and instructed him to buy some paint and apply it to the shingles. Daddy felt that buying paint was a terrible waste of this money. Therefore, instead of making the trip to town, Daddy went to the garage and removed all the cans of leftover paint that he could find. Then he went onto the roof and painted all the shingles. My grandfather got home after dark that night and left before the sun rose the next morning. A couple of days past and Grandpa hadn't seen the roof. However, Daddy's good fortune could not last forever. On Sunday, as usual, the family went to church. When they returned home the atmosphere was much different to an ordinary Sunday. The neighbors had gathered in the street and seemed to be staring at their house. At first, Grandpa was unaware of what was going on. Finally, he looked in the direction that seemed to be capturing everyone's interest and received an unpleasant surprise. Daddy had painted all the shingles in different colors! The roof of his house looked like a giant quilt! Once my grandpa realized what had happened, he gave Daddy the spanking of a lifetime and demanded to know what happened to the money he was given.

"I took everyone to the movies." Daddy said unapologetically.

"Well, I hope you enjoyed it!" Grandpa said, giving Daddy's butt another smack.

Since Grandpa refused to waste money, the roof looked like a quilt for over a year, until it was time to weather it again.

# A Sight for Sore Eyes

Daddy never graduated from high school. To make up for his lack of formal education, Daddy made a habit of reading everything he could get his hands on. In fact, he read so much that he understood the United States intended to enter World War II long before most people.

At the time, my grandma Evelyn was sick, and Daddy desperately wanted to stay in Chicago to take care of her. In May of 1941, to avoid being drafted, he enlisted in the National Guard. He, like so many others, assumed that the National Guard was there to "guard the nation" —- WRONG! The National Guard was usually trained faster than any of the other armed forces, so they were sent first to cover all war zones. In December of 1941, the United States entered the war, and Daddy, having just finished boot camp, was promptly sent overseas. He was stationed in India and began his duties as a cook. His tour of duty was to last thirteen months and his primary responsibility was to fly food into The Black Sheep Squad every week.

While he was overseas, Daddy discovered that he had an ear for languages. By the end of his thirteen-month tour, he could speak all 27 Hindi dialects and was the only one who could successfully act as a universal translator. Because of this special talent, his assignment was prolonged a few months, then a few more months, and then a few months more.

In the end, he served overseas for four and a half years before finally returning home. He returned to The United States via California. The first thing he did after landing was to call his mother. "Mom," he announced excitedly, "I'm coming home and I'm all right." Expecting an enthusiastic response, he was shocked to hear his mother say, "I'll believe it when I see it."

On the remainder of the trip home, Daddy contemplated why my grandma had been so short with him over the phone. He got his answer soon enough. Not more than a few seconds after he walked through the door, Grandma made him strip down to his underwear. Then, she spent several minutes searching every inch of his body. She seemed to have a desperate need to prove to herself that he wasn't hiding some kind of war injury. Once she was satisfied that Daddy was truly all right, she sat down and cried, letting loose a flood of four and a half years' worth of unshed tears.

# A Match Made in Illinois

Since he was a teenager, Daddy had known the woman he wanted to marry. Her name was Florence Scott, the girl next door. Daddy lovingly called her "Scottie." For the first 18 years that they lived next door to each other, nothing developed beyond friendship. Although my Aunt Helen claims that it was obvious that the two of them would be hitched one day. When they were kids, Daddy took to tying his pillow onto the handlebars of his bike before giving Mama a ride to school. When Grandpa Robert asked him why he did this, he simply responded, "Because the handlebars hurt Scottie's bum."

One year, Mama purchased two Valentine cards for a penny, the only ones she could afford. The first one she gave to her mama, the second one she put in Daddy's mailbox. When he received the card, he hopped over the fence separating their properties to thank her, and that started their courtship.

Mama was a well-educated woman. One of her favorite things to do was crossword puzzles. Mama got Daddy hooked on doing the puzzles too. Every day he would read the newspaper and then do the crossword. When he was sent overseas, Mama started saving all the crossword puzzles from the daily paper. The newspaper always printed the solution to the previous day's puzzle in the current issue. She took great pains to keep all the papers in sequential order. When Daddy came home, Mama handed him four and a half years' worth of crossword puzzles!

Although she didn't send the crossword puzzles to Daddy while he was away, they did correspond regularly. One of the best little gifts Mama sent Daddy was a small collection of magic tricks. Unfortunately, the instructions had been censored by the War Office. When he received them, the paper looked like Swiss cheese! Daddy took the opportunity to teach himself the tricks and created a few of his own. He was known for the performances he put on for his fellow soldiers.

Shortly after his return home, they started talking about getting married. However, there was one giant obstacle that threatened their plans. Daddy was a Catholic and Mama was a Protestant. Grandma Evelyn was set in her beliefs and didn't want Daddy to marry outside the faith, so she was against the match from the beginning. As it turned out, fate was on his side.

When he was overseas, he contracted viral malaria. He started taking Quinine in high doses which, at the time, was thought to be the only cure for malaria. Unfortunately, one common side effect of the drug was sterility. When Daddy told his mother that the treatment for malaria had left him sterile, things started working out for him. Since Mama had a tipped uterus and had been told by her doctor that it would be nearly impossible for her to conceive, children were not a factor in the union. Grandma consented to the marriage because, as she told Daddy, "I'm not going to waste a good Catholic woman on you." My parents were married in 1946.

A few months into their marriage Mama started feeling a little ill. She made an appointment with her doctor. After a thorough exam, the doctor sat back and gave her a quizzical look. After a moment he asked, "What do *you* think is wrong with you, Florence?"

Mama answered, "If I didn't know better, I would think I was pregnant. But I can't be, I'm sterile."

He responded nonchalantly, "Tell that to the baby."

When the news came out that Mama was pregnant, my grandma was furious. She was sure that my parents had lied to her about their conditions. In truth, they'd been operating on assumptions. Neither had officially been diagnosed sterile but their deceit wasn't intentional. My grandma was ready to disown Daddy and to have him excommunicated from the Church. Mama tried to make amends, but her mother-in-law couldn't be reasoned with. Finally, Mama converted to Catholicism to smooth Grandma's rumpled feathers.

As Mama's pregnancy progressed, she discovered that she was pregnant with twins. She carried the babies to full-term, but her tipped uterus made labor extremely difficult. In the end, my brother George survived but his twin did not.

The doctors told Mama that it would be in her best interest to avoid another pregnancy. She was warned that each new birth would be a risk to her life. Although Mama believed this to be true, she didn't listen because she had enough love for an army of children. Consequently, Mama continued to grow her family. In addition to losing George's twin, she miscarried twice. In total, she had six children that survived: George, Juanita, Mike, Saro, Evelyn (me), and Frances. After eight pregnancies, she finally decided her family was complete.

# Photos
# 1910s to 1940s

Back Row: Lawrence Melvin, James & "Lottie" Parry, Lloyd & Dema Scott
Second Row: Lily Melvin, Will Boger, Dora Boger, Orvil Boger, Leona Boger Hoag
Front Row: Baby Dorothy, Baby Florence (late 1919)

*Grandpa Lawrence Melvin &*
*Grandma Lily Melvin (circa 1914)*

*Grandma Dema Scott &*
*Grandpa Lloyd Scott (circa 1916)*

*Mama (Florence) &*
*Grandma Dema (July 1, 1921)*

Daddy (George, Age 13) &
Grandpa Robert (1934)

Grandpa Robert Sluppick, Grandma Evelyn Nielsen Sluppick (Daddy's Parents, 1946)

Daddy (George) – Home from the War (1945)

My Parents' wedding (1946). Left to Right: Bud Fry (Best Man), George Sluppick (Daddy), Florence Scott (Mama), Margaret Fry (Daddy's sister, Matron of Honor)

# 1950s-1960s

# The Unsweet Life

When I was 14 months old, Mama took me to the doctor because I wasn't gaining weight. The doctor took one look at me and said I wasn't getting enough to eat. He believed that Mama was starving me and threatened to alert the police. When Mama told Daddy what the doctor said, he was furious at this accusation. He marched into the doctor's office, grabbed the doctor, pushed him against the wall and exclaimed, "How dare you tell my wife that she is abusing my children. I want to know what is wrong with my baby girl! NOW!" The doctor responded, "I'm sorry, Mr. Sluppick, we really don't know." Daddy shouted, "Then that's what you tell my wife!"

After some tests, I was diagnosed with celiac disease. In 1954, this was thought to be caused by the inability to digest sugar, which can result in malnutrition. They discovered that my pancreas was the size of a four-year-old's. This disease caused me to appear sick all the time, and when I did become sick it hit me ten times worse. As a result of my diagnosis, I was forbidden to eat sweets. We lived in a neighborhood where everyone knew everyone, and my condition was common knowledge. Every Halloween my neighbors gave me special gifts instead of candy. I would get treats such as pencils, knitted mittens, and fruit. I remember one lady would give me ten shiny new pennies every year.

Since I was diagnosed with celiac disease at a young age, I hadn't been exposed to many sugary treats, therefore, I didn't really miss them. My loss truly hit me just before my third birthday. Juanita's birthday is four days before mine. That year she had a birthday party and had invited around ten friends. When it came time to have cake and ice cream, Mama brought out a chocolate cake with chocolate icing. Daddy had purchased me a Bosc pear. This type of pear was an expensive piece of fruit, but I didn't care. I really wanted a piece of cake. I took that pear and threw it as hard as I could and screamed, "Don't want no damned pear." I watched as Daddy chased that pear across the yard. After all, he wasn't about to let it go to waste.

When my birthday came a few days later, my parents had planned a birthday party for me too. All the neighborhood kids were going to be there. I was still so upset about the pear that I refused to go to the party. Since my birthday is in the middle of July, my parents had turned on the sprinklers for the children to run through. Everyone was having a great time and Daddy was upset that I wasn't there. He walked upstairs, picked me up, and carried me to the party like I was a football. When we got downstairs, I sat in the corner with my arms crossed, refusing to celebrate.

My mood changed when the crowd started singing "Happy Birthday" and suddenly, Daddy came through the crowd with a huge watermelon that had been cut in half, which he had chilled for several days. He stuck four candles in my "cake," three for my years and one *to grow on*. It was the perfect dessert for a hot day, and I insisted on a watermelon birthday cake until I was ten years old.

A few months after my third birthday, when I'd had enough of my restrictions, I snuck into the kitchen and climbed onto the counter. I grabbed the jar of peanut butter out of the cupboard. I was sitting there sticking a spoon in the jar and eating the peanut butter with delight when Daddy walked in and caught me. He asked in shock, "Evelyn, what are you eating?" With my mouth full of the sugary goodness, I answered, "Nuffin." He didn't discipline me though. The stomachache I got was punishment enough.

The next time that I got extremely sick (after the peanut butter scandal) wasn't from my own rebellion. It was my brother's fault! My brother, George, came home from visiting a friend, and later discovered that his friend had been contagious with chicken pox. George came back infected and, subsequentially, came down with a mild form of scarlet fever. He recovered a few days later. I, on the other hand, suffered much longer. I became infected with chicken pox too and, soon after, scarlet fever. My fever rose to 105°F and didn't decrease for five days. When my fever reached its peak, my parents rushed me to the hospital. I was isolated in the Emergency Room until my fever broke. Every few minutes, the doctors would pack me in ice, and a few minutes later the ice would be slush and my fever would still be raging. Since a brain will start to fry at 106°F, the doctor told Mama that I was most likely going to die and if, by some miracle, I didn't, I would "be an idiot."

I stayed in the hospital for three weeks. During that time, my house was quarantined, and all my clothing was burned. Luckily, I made a full recovery with all my wits about me. However, the scarlet fever caused me to lose my hair. Then, by the same doctor,

Mama was told that I would probably be bald for the rest of my life, or I'd have a fever streak *if* my hair grew back. Mama was heartbroken by this news. Luckily, the doctor was wrong again. When my hair started to grow back a few months later, it was nothing more than peach fuzz, but it was just enough to say that I *wasn't* bald and there was no evidence of a fever streak. It stayed like that for another two years. Around the age of five, my hair started to grow again at a normal rate.

When we were young, Mama gave my siblings their haircuts, but she was reluctant to cut mine. The first time my brother, George, went to the barber shop, it was a big event. He came home with a perfect professional haircut. As soon as he walked through the door, he saw me and asked, "Evelyn, do you want to play barber?" "Sure!" I said enthusiastically. My brother immediately started cutting my hair. After a few minutes, he declared that it was "a little uneven" and cut some more. A few minutes later and it was still "a little uneven." About 30 minutes passed with my hair hitting the floor before George said, "Oops, I'm going to go out and play."

Mama was ironing in the other room. I went in to see her, and she smiled at me and said, "Who's little boy are you?" I answered, surprised she didn't know me, "Mama it's me!" Then, she almost fainted.

When I was six years old, during a routine checkup, my parents were informed that I was no longer suffering from celiac disease. My body had caught up with the size of my pancreas, so they didn't expect I'd have any further issues. Upon hearing this news, Daddy put my siblings and I in the car and he drove us to the nearest bakery. I couldn't believe my eyes. There were so many chocolate cakes, brownies, and cookies. I was even more surprised when

Daddy told me that it was my special day and, since I could eat sugar now, I could have anything I wanted. Much to the disappointment of my siblings, I was the sole recipient of this treat. My eyes landed on the biggest sugar cookie I'd ever seen in my life. It was, easily, as big as my face. As we drove home, I devoured my cookie and refused to share, even though my brothers and sisters were begging for a bite. At one point, I remember looking over and seeing Daddy cry. This was a rare sight, and, at the time, I couldn't understand why he was crying. After all, the cookie was really good.

This period in my life was probably harder on Mama than myself. She didn't want to remember these painful circumstances. During this time, she'd refused to have my picture taken. Years later, after I was married with children of my own, I was visiting Mama, and we were sifting through old boxes when I came across a picture of me and Daddy. When I showed it to Mama, she became livid. Apparently, against Mama's wishes, Daddy had been determined to have a picture with me. He had bundled me up like "Nanook of the North" and carried me outside. I had on so many layers that all that could be seen of me were my two little eyes.

Mama may have hated that Daddy had taken that picture, but it will always be one of my favorites. I hung a copy in my hallway and, every now and then, it still brings tears to my eyes.

# Up in Flames

I was born in Chicago, Illinois, but I grew up in Memphis, Tennessee. As a child, I often wondered what prompted our move to the South. As an adult, I finally decided to ask Mama. I was amazed at the story she told.

On our property in Illinois, Daddy owned and ran a garage that mainly serviced large vehicles, such as semi-trucks. He became well known for his skills and was recruited by the Frank Hough Construction Company to run their operation in Memphis.

In April 1957, when I was about three and a half years old, Mama and Daddy left town to search for a house in our new hometown. While they were gone, my siblings and I were in the care of a babysitter. The woman, who had children of her own, was primarily responsible for Fran and me since we were the youngest of the bunch.

One day, Juanita, George, and Mike were returning home from school and, just as they were reaching the property, George must've seen smoke since he screamed, "The garage is on fire!"

Without hesitation, George and Mike ran into the house, saw that Fran and I were sleeping, scooped us up and, with Juanita, took us to the neighbor's house down the hill. In the hours that followed, firemen attempted to save our home but to no avail. We lost everything. In a newspaper article a few days later, Mama humbly stated, "The Good Lord saw fit to save all of my children and none of their underwear." After the commotion and shock died down, it occurred to everyone that no one knew where the babysitter was, and they never saw her again. Also, the cause of the fire was never established.

Our family was too large for any one household to take us in. Consequently, we were spread out among several caring families in the community. During the days that followed, we experienced a wealth of generosity from friends and strangers. There was an overwhelming sense of shared loss in our little town. Gifts were left for our family on the doorsteps of the different homes we were occupying. One gift that Mama heartwarmingly recalled was a laundry basket overflowing with goodies. The basket contained a coffee pot and a pound of coffee with a note inside that read, "All is not lost if you can make a pot of coffee." In addition to the coffee, there was a dish service for eight, pots, pans, and silverware, among other things. All the items were mismatched, which led Mama to believe that this perfect stranger had raided every thrift store in town.

As Mama shared this story, she remarked that, ironically, the house in Illinois was burning down at the same time they had been signing the documents for the new property in Tennessee. I took that opportunity to confide in her as well. I revealed that I used to have a reoccurring dream as a little girl that I finally understood.

In the dream, I was standing outside surrounded by people I loved and staring up into a barely recognizable structure that was covered in flames. But even as I stood there watching the obvious ending of a life I knew, I had a warm feeling and a sense of hope that held strong, even in the direst of situations.

# Playing House

Many of the people I knew growing up might have thought that I was Miss Goody Two-Shoes because I rarely went to parties or did anything against the rules. Therefore, I'm sure it would shock them to know that I nearly had a prison record.

I was five years old and one of the neighborhood boys and I were outside playing. We wound up in the yard of another neighbor whose family was on vacation. A few hours later, there was a knock at my front door. Mama answered it and became immediately concerned. In front of her stood a police officer and, on the other end of his handcuffs, none other than yours truly. Of course, it didn't occur to me at the time that my little wrist could easily have slipped out of the cuffs. But I stood there, my arm stretched as high as it would go, and I waited to be punished.

"What happened?" Mama asked in shock. The alarm in her voice brought Daddy to the door as well.

The officer replied, "Someone phoned the station about some activity in the house across the street. The lights were on, so they called us. When we arrived at the scene, we caught her and a little boy in your neighbor's kitchen. They were playing house."

Mama was mortified. I shudder to think of the thoughts that must have crossed her mind. I stood terrified as she uttered, "I'm so sorry officer. We'll be sending her straight to her room without supper." The officer must have sensed her embarrassment, so he decided to clarify his announcement.

The officer proclaimed, "No ma'am, I mean they were 'playing house.' He was sitting at the kitchen table wearing a sports coat and reading a newspaper. She was wearing an apron, pouring him cereal, and talking about needing a new dishwasher."

Daddy began laughing so hard that he nearly passed out. Daddy thanked the officer as I was being released from my captivity. Once he closed the front door, he knelt to my level and said, "How about we go out for a burger?"

Mama tried to stop him. "No, that's going to send her the wrong message."

To which he simply replied, "It was their fault they didn't lock the door."

# For the Love of...

I will never forget the first man I fell in love with. He was tall, dark, and handsome. He was brave and daring. He was attentive and courteous. He was everything a girl could hope for. When we met, I was five years old. His name was... Zorro.

I made a date with Zorro every Saturday morning, and I wouldn't have missed it for the world. One Saturday morning, as always, I was sitting on my couch watching Zorro heroically fighting the bad guys, when halfway through the show my brother Mike walked into the living room and sat on the footstool right in front of me. Figuring that he hadn't seen me sitting there, I slid over to the other side of the couch. Then Mike got up, moved the footstool and, *again*, sat in front of me. Once again, I shifted my position without saying anything to him and, once again, he moved to block my view. Since Mike often picked on me, I understood what he was doing.

"Move, Mike." I finally said, attempting to hide my frustration.

"No." he replied nonchalantly.

Stifling my growing anger, I moved again and, a few seconds later, so did Mike.

"Move, Mike." I firmly requested, again.

"No."

Determined not to miss *Zorro*, I got up and went straight into the kitchen to grab Mama's cast iron frying pan. I casually walked back out to the living room and sat back down on the couch. Holding my weapon with intent to cause bodily damage, if necessary, I declared in my most threatening voice, "Move, *Mike*, or you'll be sorry."

"No." he replied, either oblivious to my irritation or, perhaps, fueled by it.

Feeling that I had given him a full warning, I hoisted that pan as high as I could and brought it down square on top of Mike's head. My mother rounded the corner just in time to see Mike fall over like a bag of rocks. Mama screamed at me, "What did you do?!" As she ran toward Mike, I started defending myself, but she was having none of it. She thought for sure that I had killed him. He *survived* the blow. I, on the other hand, might as well have died. Mama grounded me from a *month* of *Zorro* episodes!

I held that punishment against Mike for years after that. After all, Mama wouldn't have been so harsh with me if she had listened to my explanation that Mike had instigated the whole thing. In my five-year-old mind, it was terribly unfair. Luckily, even a month of separation didn't dampen the love I had for the masked avenger. A love that has stood the test of time and still holds strong to this day.

# The Doctor is in

When I was about six years old, I received a nursing play kit for Christmas. Among other essentials, it contained band-aids, a blood pressure gauge, a little reflex hammer, and even a plastic thermometer. I loved this present, but my sister, Fran, loved it even more. It got to the point that the toy was hardly mine anymore. Fran carried it with her wherever she went. After a while, no one noticed the kit in her tiny little hand because, like socks or shoes, it became a normal part of her daily uniform.

Her favorite piece in the set was the plastic thermometer. She would walk around for hours at a time taking everyone and everything's temperature. This is no exaggeration either. She stuck that thermometer in the plants, the dog's mouth, the dirt, the couch cushions... you name it. This was a relatively harmless past time (unless you were unlucky enough to be the next patient after the toilet water), so Mama never discouraged her. Then one day while I was starting to doze off on my bed, Fran decided I needed a check-up. With one swift move, she took that thermometer and jammed it into my ear. *OH THE PAIN!* I hadn't seen what happened, but I knew that it couldn't be good. Blood began dripping down the side of my face as I ran down the hall to Mama. The look on her face when she saw me made me cry even harder. She immediately rushed me into the bathroom and started to clean out my ear with peroxide. It turned out that Fran had popped my eardrum. However, if I thought the popped eardrum hurt, the peroxide hurt a thousand times worse. After Mama got the bleeding to slow down a bit, she took me to the hospital. The doctor told us that once the wound healed there would be some scar tissue around my eardrum, and I would most likely lose hearing in that ear.

The next day I was sitting next to Daddy, and I was crying because my ear still hurt so badly. Daddy, who was smoking a cigar, lifted me onto his knee and said, "I'll make it all better." He took a puff on his cigar and slowly exhaled the smoke directly into my injured ear. To my surprise, the warmth of the cigar smoke soothed the pain. For three months, as my ear healed, Daddy would pull me onto his lap and repeat this procedure. It became my daily therapy, and I looked forward to it. Once my recovery was complete, we discovered that, although the injury did result in some scar tissue surrounding my eardrum, I didn't lose any of my hearing.

I became less tolerant of smokers as I got older. However, when I catch a whiff of the familiar scent of cigar smoke, I think of Daddy and I get a warm feeling inside of being cared for, loved, and safe.

# The Starving Armenians

When I was little, my family belonged to the "Clean Plate Society" and my father might as well have been the society's president. In his eyes, it was considered a waste to leave even one morsel of food on your plate. Daddy was famous for the guilt trip he laid on my siblings and me about how grateful we should be that we had food to eat, unlike "The Starving Armenians." On occasion, this mentality resulted in everyone being excused from the table except for the child who was still picking at their food. That child was left sitting at the dining room table alone until every bite was consumed. Often, we could entice the dog to help us finish off our supper. However, sometimes that didn't work.

One day, when I was seven and Fran was six, we overheard Mama say that we were going to have liver & onions for supper. Fran hated liver. As always, when the meal was over for us, Fran was left abandoned to finish her liver alone. About a half an hour later she shouted, "Okay Daddy, I'm done." Daddy went to inspect her dish and then she was excused from the table.

Three weeks later, there was a knock at our door. Daddy opened the door to a confused mailman. “Hello Mr. Sluppick. I was hoping you could help me out with something,” the mailman requested, “Down at the office, we have a bet going. We received this package about three weeks ago. We are all very curious to see what’s in it.” Daddy was handed a taped-up shoebox, which had an awful, disgusting odor emanating from it. Daddy opened the package which was addressed to: “The Starving Armenians.” It contained a rotting liver dinner. Since Fran had been learning how to address mail in school, she properly included our return address on the label. Mama must have laughed for a solid hour. Daddy never again lectured us about “The Starving Armenians.” Thanks to Fran, he also never again left us alone at the table to finish our supper.

# Tootsie Role

Growing up in the South in the middle of the $20^{th}$ century was often an eye-opening experience. Segregation and discrimination were commonplace and was rarely challenged. Fortunately, in my household, we were taught that discrimination was wrong, and that God cut everyone from the same cloth.

When I was six years old, a black girl was placed into my class. Her name was Tootsie. Sadly, none of the other kids wanted to play with her. When the teacher asked me if Tootsie could sit with me, I was quick to accept. That first day at recess, while Tootsie and I walked through the playground, I was shocked to witness what transpired. The children in our class came running up to Tootsie and began biting her. Later, I discovered that Tootsie's last name was Role, and the children had wanted to see if she tasted like a tootsie roll candy. By the time we left school, Tootsie was covered in red swollen bite marks.

That night, Tootsie and her dad came over to our house. While Daddy and Mr. Role were downstairs, talking, Tootsie and

I were sent upstairs to play. I remember hearing Tootsie's dad ranting and raving. He seemed to get more furious by the minute. Finally, I heard Daddy interrupt Mr. Role and calmly say, "Just remember that your little black child is up there playing with my little white child." That seemed to diffuse the situation and Mr. Role never again yelled at my daddy.

Tootsie and I became good friends. Unfortunately, this was at the expense of my other friendships. Many of my classmates spent their energy shouting various names and insults at Tootsie and me, most of which I didn't fully comprehend at the time.

One afternoon I came home and said to Daddy, "Did you know that Tootsie is an n-word?" (Of course, at that time, I had used the real word). He slapped me across my face so hard that I thought my head was going to fall off. As his hand made contact, he shouted, "*NEVER* say that word!" I didn't understand what I had said to make him so angry. I had only repeated what my classmates had called her, and I thought Daddy could explain why a word could cause such hatred. I felt the tears running down my cheek as the mark where Daddy had slapped me started to sting. He left without explaining himself, and I never used that word again in my life.

Tootsie and I went through the rest of our school years together and were practically inseparable. Eventually, more of the students at our school began to accept her and we had our own little circle of friends. As we grew older, she complained more passionately about her name. She told me that it was demeaning and that she was going to have it legally changed.

That summer she went to a family reunion and, when she returned, her attitude about her name was completely different. I asked her why she seemed so attached to her name suddenly. She explained that her grandmother had heard her complaining about her name. Her grandmother took her aside and told her she was named after her great-grandmother. Apparently, her great-grandmother had been a slave and the first thing she did after being freed was to take a walk outside. While contemplating her new freedom, she noticed the distant sound of a train passing. She recognized the "toot" "toot" "toot" of the train's whistle as a beautiful, *free* sound and she symbolically changed her "slave name" to her chosen *free name* "Toot"-sie.

# The King and I

I grew up in Memphis, Tennessee, just a short distance from Graceland. Daddy did business with Elvis Presley and my brother George worked on his cars. Still, there are three instances where I remember him personally.

The first time I was extremely young. The local A&P had a special on milk; a half gallon was 25 cents, but it was only one per customer. Daddy never could resist a bargain. To beat the system, Daddy brought the whole family down to the market. I'm sure it must have been a sight in the checkout line. Mama headed up our little army, followed by my three brothers, my two sisters and me, with Daddy bringing up the caboose. Each one of us was holding a half gallon of milk and a shiny new quarter.

While we waited, the man behind Daddy said, "Hello, Mr. Sluppick. How are you doing?" They began talking and I paid no attention. The man was Elvis. The only part of their conversation that I remember was when he referred to us. "So, who are these children?" To which Daddy replied with pride, "These are *my* children."

The next instance that stands out in my mind occurred during Christmastime while I was in high school. One of the girls in my class asked Fran and me if we'd like to come to church with her to hear her choir sing. We were delighted. During the service, the minister requested that one of the parishioners lead the group in a song. The parishioner was Elvis, and the song was *The Battle Hymn of the Republic.* Elvis stood at the head of the choir in his black suit with a white shirt and black tie. He sang with 300 back-up hummers. He sang with such passion that, as we were leaving, Fran leaned over to me and said, "Let's go kill us some damn Yankees." She was all fired up until I reminded her that we were born in Illinois — so *we* were some "damn Yankees."

The last instance that stands out to me involves one of my cousins. She was visiting us and was enthralled by how close we lived to The King of Rock and Roll. At the time, Graceland was not protected by much security. When she wanted to go to Elvis' house, it was an easy request to fill. My cousin, a few friends, and I drove through the front gate, right up his driveway, and parked within feet of his front door. My cousin was in awe.

As we were walking toward the front door, my cousin spotted Elvis' orange tree and promptly started to climb. She told me later that she believed that Elvis' orange would taste different somehow. As luck would have it, she would never know. The fruit was just within her reach when she fell out of the tree. Elvis saw it happen from an upstairs window and rushed outside. He leaned over her to make sure she was all right and she began screaming. Elvis then scooped her up and put her in his car. He drove her straight to the hospital and the rest of us followed behind.

After a thorough examination, we discovered that she had merely broken her leg. She felt miserable and embarrassed for the rest of the day. The next day her mood improved drastically when Elvis Presley walked into her room with a bouquet of flowers. It seems he felt partially responsible for her fall.

When she was being discharged, the family was informed that the hospital bill was already taken care of. Mama confided in me years later about a conversation she'd had with Elvis. He had insisted on covering the hospital expenses. After the incident, Mama pulled Elvis aside and asked him, "Can I tell them now? So, they can thank you? They've been wondering who paid the bill."

Elvis then shook his head and replied, "If they need to thank someone, they can thank the doctors and thank the nurses. All I did was write a check."

# It's Magic

My Daddy died when I was ten years old, so I didn't get that much time with him. Although I have fond memories of him, I also remember a time when I wasn't thrilled that we were related.

When I was seven years old, my school was holding the annual career day, and Daddy had agreed to come speak to my class. He was a salesman, and, to a child, this was about the most boring job a person could have. I practically died thinking of Daddy speaking to my classmates. I wondered, *what's he going to do? Write a receipt? Take inventory?* I dreaded the upcoming career day.

To my horror, the day arrived, and the earth hadn't opened to swallow me whole. I was going to have to endure Daddy's presentation. As his turn got closer, my heart sank deeper. Then, when he finally stood in front of the class, I braced myself for torture.

He began speaking about the importance of keeping your customer interested in the product you are selling. He told us that, "you must get your customers to like you. If you can get them interested in you as a person," he said, "then you can sell them anything." I will forever remember this speech because of what he was doing as he was talking.

As soon as Daddy started, he simultaneously mesmerized my class with magic. Not figuratively but literally. It was more interesting than the "sales receipt" lecture that I had been dreading, but it still bored me. I loved his magic tricks, but I had seen them all before.

In one of these tricks, he took a rope and tied it into several separate knots. He then cut the rope at each knot and placed each section of rope into different pockets. He put one knot into each pocket of his pants, one in each front pocket of his jacket, and one in his inside jacket pocket. He had one knot left over. He called a little girl to the front of the class and put the last knot in her pocket.

"Now make sure you keep ahold of that knot," Daddy told her seriously. My classmate, determined to keep the knot safe, put her hand over her pocket. Then Daddy started spinning her around in circles. After several seconds, he looked at her, and asked, "Do you still have the knot?"

"Yes," she said with confidence.

"You better check," he told her.

Then, from her little pocket, she removed the entire length of rope with no knots in sight. My classmates charged to the front of the class and ripped Daddy's suit to shreds, looking for the knots that he hid within his jacket and pants. He had sacrificed his perfectly good suit- what a maroon!

He continued talking after the children had settled down again. At one point, he turned to our teacher and asked, "Sister Ethel Bert, doesn't that bother you?"

"What?" she asked, confused.

Then, Daddy reached over and pulled a quarter out of her ear. Sister Ethel Bert walked around the rest of the day with her finger in her ear searching for more lost treasure.

He finally grabbed my attention when he began a trick that I had never seen before. He continued to talk about sales while he pulled out a brand-new deck of cards. He broke the seal on the cards and divided them into two piles- black and red. He then placed the box on top of the two piles. He covered the whole thing with one of Mama's old dish towels, which he called his "magic cloth," and then he said his magic words. "Diggy Diggy." When he removed the cloth, he revealed that the cards were nestled back in their box. It was even more amazing when he removed the cards again and revealed they had been shuffled together in alternating shades, red-black-red-black-red-black, all the way through the deck.

The next parent to talk to us was a fireman. He began his speech with, "Gee, Mr. Sluppick, how am I supposed to top that?"

Daddy continued to develop new magic tricks throughout the rest of his life. He had a signature trick where he would have a volunteer pick a playing card from a deck and he would take a Polaroid of the back of the chosen card. Then, when the Polaroid developed, it revealed a negative of the volunteer's card! We never knew how he did it since a "Magician never reveals his secrets." However, when Daddy got close to the end of his life. He told Mama, "Sell the trick. It'll set you and the children up for life." Unfortunately, in his declined mental state, he didn't realize he'd never explained how the trick was accomplished. After he passed, they held a contest through the local papers with a monetary reward if someone could figure it out. No one ever did.

# Out to Lunch

Living in the South during the early 1960s was challenging when you didn't share the same prejudices as your neighbors. My parents felt all people were equal. They worked and socialized with people from all backgrounds and races. Even though some segregation practices were legally banned, the law was rarely enforced.

I remember a day when Daddy took Mama and all of us children to Walgreens for lunch. At a table outside, Daddy saw one of his coworkers who happened to be a black man. Daddy sat us all down next to his friend. Daddy and his friend became engaged in animated conversation.

Daddy tried multiple times to get the waitress's attention so he could place our order. He soon realized that she was deliberately ignoring him. When he finally walked inside and confronted her, she stated vehemently that she couldn't take his order while he was "sitting with *that* man." He didn't want to create a scene or embarrass his friend, so he ordered eight cheeseburgers, eight fries, and eight Cokes to go. I'm sure she thought he was a troublemaker.

She was happy to fulfill his request quickly so that he could leave. She was in for a rude awakening.

One of Daddy's biggest pet peeves was people telling him what he could and couldn't do. After he got our order, he walked back to the seat next to his friend and sat down. To the waitress's horror, we stayed and ate our meal out of those little To-Go boxes.

# Chatty Cathy

I was seven years old when Chatty Cathy was introduced to the world. She was the first talking doll and I had to have her. I knew that I would die if I didn't get her for Christmas that year, so I started making my sales pitch early.

I managed to get the name Chatty Cathy into every conversation I had with my parents. I ate, slept, and breathed Chatty Cathy. Everything I did revolved around owning that doll. I even prayed every night that my parents would fork over the small fortune to put her in my possession.

I was so excited when Christmas morning came. I knew that all my efforts must have paid off and, by the end of the morning, I would have Chatty Cathy in my arms. Every gift I opened was a small disappointment since it didn't contain the gift I really wanted. After opening my last non-Chatty Cathy gift, I sat stunned. How could my parents have missed all the hints I had dropped? How could they have left me Chatty Cathy-less?!

I sulked as my siblings played with their new toys. I was determined to send a clear message that my parents had dropped the ball. When Daddy called me upstairs, I stomped up every step grumbling under my breath. I was angry and frustrated and sad. Once I reached the top of the stairs I sat down in a big huff. I heard Daddy come up behind me and then I heard... *"Hi, I'm Chatty Cathy."*

In shock, I swiftly turned around, successfully tripping myself. I fell down the stairs, rolling over each one until I hit the bottom landing. From that vantage point, I could see Daddy running down the stairs with my new doll in his hands. Mama freaked out and we rushed to the hospital. To everyone's surprise, I didn't get a concussion. Regardless of my brush with death, that was my best Christmas ever.

# Nurse in Training

During the summer when I turned eight years old, Daddy was already chronically sick. He'd had a stroke a few years earlier and, as a result, his health deteriorated in multiple ways. Mama was working full-time at the hospital, Fran was too young for major responsibilities, and my older siblings had their own lives to deal with. Consequently, Mama assigned me the task of taking care of Daddy after school. The most important one of my responsibilities was to take detailed notes of everything Daddy did and at what times.

During the school year, we were required to hand in our assignments in cursive writing. Although classes were out for the summer, I could still hear the nuns' voices in my head about the importance of using cursive. Therefore, I used cursive to take notes about Daddy's activities. When I handed my observations to Mama, she took me aside and said calmly, "I can't read these notes. From now on, I need you to start printing everything. It is very important that I can read *everything* that you write down." For the rest of the summer, just as Mama instructed, I threw cursive writing out of the window and wrote everything in print.

On the first day of the next school year, the nuns were going over the school rules, and they reminded the students, "It is very important that we can read everything that you turn in." Since Mama found it difficult to read my cursive writing, I completed my homework in printed writing.

After I handed in my first few assignments, a note was sent home to my parents stating that I wasn't completing the assignments in cursive as required. When Mama read the note, I began to cry. I explained to her that they had told me to write clearly.

Mama went to my school the next day and explained the situation to the nuns. Unfortunately, the nuns showed little sympathy. They told Mama, "At this school, we use cursive. If Evelyn prints her assignments, she will lose points and she will fail penmanship."

Mama returned home, having accomplished nothing. She told Daddy what happened so that I would not have to explain my bad grade to him. Afterward, he told me, "It's not the end of the world." With the consent of my parents, I continued to print my assignments. I did, in fact, fail penmanship that year.

In the winter after my ninth birthday, I was still taking care of Daddy. By then, Daddy had been sick for about a year and a half. I took the job as his nurse seriously. One day, when school was closed due to excessive snow, I was spending some free time out in the backyard. We had, what seemed to me, a small forest on our property. I was standing among the trees when I thought I heard Daddy calling my name. Worried that he was in pain, I took off running toward the house. I ran through the trees, across the snow-covered lawn, up the porch, into the house, and all the way up the stairs to Daddy's room, without stopping. I went from the freezing cold outside to our nicely heated home within seconds.

By the time I arrived in Daddy's room, the drastic and sudden temperature change to my body had caused tears to run down my cheeks. In addition, the urgency with which I ran had left me out of breath. As I exploded into his room, I quickly asked, "Daddy... do you want me?" Unexpectedly, Daddy began to cry. Then he pulled me onto his lap and said, with remarkable calmness and love, "Of course I want you." At that moment, I realized that he hadn't called for me, but rather, his voice had rung through my imagination.

For the rest of the night, Daddy held me closely to him while we watched television in his bedroom. That event was a real treat, and a memory that I will cherish always. I never had the heart to tell him that it was my fear for *him* that brought me into his room that day, not fear for myself.

# Daddy, is That You?

Christmas has always been my favorite time of year. When I was a young girl, I used to love sitting in Daddy's lap and hearing about Santa Claus coming down the chimney and leaving us presents under the tree. I never questioned the logic of this task.

In 1962, I was nine years old. Daddy, even with his health problems, continued the tradition of telling us stories of old St. Nick on Christmas Eve. That year, after we put our milk and cookies out for Santa, we kissed Mama and Daddy goodnight, and we went to our bedrooms. My brother Saro, sister Fran, and I had no intention of sleeping though. The three of us were determined to meet Santa face-to-face.

Around ten o'clock, long after Mama and Daddy had gone to bed, the three of us sneaked downstairs and hid under the dining room table. We had a long tablecloth that stopped just short of the floor, so we were well hidden. We weren't there for more than 30 minutes when we heard footsteps on the staircase.

It wasn't Santa though; it was Daddy walking downstairs in his bathrobe. Fran and I looked at each other and whispered, simultaneously, "*what is he doing?*" I softly added, "Daddy better get back in bed. Santa Claus won't come if he doesn't get back in bed."

Then Daddy whistled for his dog Clayton. We watched as Daddy went over to the milk and cookies, which had been sitting on the counter since about three o'clock in the afternoon. Daddy picked up the glass of milk and Fran whispered in shock, "Daddy's taking Santa's milk." Then, Clayton appeared as Daddy walked to the kitchen sink, exclaiming a low, "Ho, Ho, Ho," and poured the sour milk, which had clumped like cottage cheese, down the drain. He proceeded to the fridge and removed the milk carton. He poured a small amount of milk in the empty glass and swirled it around, allowing the milk to splash around the edges of the glass. He returned the milk carton to the fridge and walked back to the table. His attention turned to the plate of cookies that Fran and I had made, which, honestly, were more like chocolate chip rocks. Daddy proceeded, with effort, to crush the cookies. At this point, Fran whispered more emphatically, "Daddy's taking Santa's cookies!" When Daddy was satisfied the chunks were small enough, he put the plate on the ground in front of Clayton. Instead of eating the cookies, Clayton glanced at the plate and then he gave Daddy this look like, *what have I ever done to you?* "Smart Dog," Daddy said laughing. Daddy picked up the plate and threw most of the cookies away, leaving only a few crumbs. He placed the plate back on the table and scribbled a note which he laid next to the plate that read,

*"Great Milk and Cookies."*

The next thing he did was the most mystifying of all. He walked over to the fireplace nook where the wood was usually kept. He opened it up and revealed tons of presents, which he proceeded to place under the tree. After Daddy emptied the nook, he walked back upstairs. The three of us remained in our hiding place for another hour, stewing in our disbelief and trying to make sense of what had happened.

The next morning Daddy came downstairs in the *same* bathrobe bellowing, "HO, HO, HO. MERRY CHRISTMAS!" I just looked at him and, with a roll of my eyes, thought how shocking it was that he and Santa shopped at the same clothing store.

# Lucy

The one thing about Mama that I will always remember is her love for animals. She virtually ran a boarding house for strays. It really did not matter if they were sick or healthy. When they wandered onto her doorstep, they could still find a warm bed under Mama's roof. Our home was a regular Noah's Ark.

One of the many homeless animals that walked through our door was a dog that appeared to be a purebred beagle. At the time, she was around nine years old but as feisty as a puppy. Mama took one look at her and said, "She looks like a Lucy." And, thus, she was named. Lucy was an instant companion for Mama, and they soon became joined at the hip.

A few weeks after she joined our family, Lucy became ill. Without hesitation, Mama took her to the vet. At first, Mama was certain that Lucy was pregnant. The veterinarian dismissed Mama's diagnosis on the grounds that Lucy was simply too old. He insisted that Lucy was suffering from liver disease. Mama was a *human* nurse, but she thought she could recognize the symptoms of pregnancy. Nonetheless, as she left the Vet's office, she considered the fact that Lucy was the equivalent to 85 human years. She accepted the doctor's findings. Mama spent the next several days looking after Lucy and she tried to make the dog as comfortable as possible. Nothing seemed to help, and Lucy became increasingly lethargic.

Shortly after her vet visit, Lucy disappeared. In true horror movie fashion, the night was cold and rainy. Mama became frantic. She was running and searching through the yard, flashlight in hand, when Fran and I woke up.

We heard her calling in the night air, "Lucy... Lucy..."

"Mama, come inside." I called from the doorway.

"Lucy's cold," she replied with worry.

"She's got a fur coat," I stated matter-of-factly.

Mama didn't seem to find my observation amusing. Fran and I were forced to join the search and rescue mission.

Finally, about thirty minutes later, we spotted Lucy under one of the bushes in front of the house. The dog was soaked but we dared not move her. Shock stapled our feet to the wet and muddy ground. We stood in disbelief as we watched Lucy giving birth to her puppies. They were popping out so fast that none of the puppies had a chance to move before the next one landed on its head. Mama immediately ran inside and grabbed a huge turkey roaster. As soon as Lucy had finished delivering her 14 puppies, Mama began transferring them to their temporary home. She successfully rescued twelve of the little ones. Unfortunately, due to the speed at which the puppies were delivered, the first two suffocated during birth. At first, I was horrified by what Mama did next. She took the puppies into the house and placed them inside of the oven. I thought, "Great, we're having roasted dog for dinner." Later I realized that she was using the oven as an incubator. Once the puppies were settled, Mama went back outside to retrieve Lucy. She wasn't a strong woman, but she carried Lucy with little effort and placed her on the kitchen counter. The remainder of the evening was spent nursing Lucy back to health. The following day, Mama took a little trip to the Vet's office. She walked up to the doctor, placed the roaster on the counter and announced, "There's your liver disease!"

Even though the veterinarian had misdiagnosed Lucy's condition, he was right about one thing: Lucy was too old to have puppies. She was unable to nurse them or care for them. Fran and I took on this extra responsibility. Our most difficult task was their feedings which occurred every two hours. Since there were so many puppies, we would hardly be done with one cycle before we had to start all over again.

When it came time to give the puppies away, I was sad and reluctant to let them go. I had cared for them so closely that I felt as if they were my own children. However, I knew that it was not practical to assume that we could continue to provide for a dozen growing munchkins. The puppies were carbon copies of their mother, so we believed that they were purebred. Unfortunately, since Lucy came to us as a stray, we had no proof of their breeding. Without proper papers, we felt that we could not sell the puppies in good conscious. We gave them away free of charge. At the time, I volunteered at the local Veteran's hospital. I was able to advertise the puppies, and they were all quickly placed in good homes. Lucy, on the other hand, remained by Mama's side for another ten years.

# The Voice is On, But Nobody is Home

Over the years, Mama took many cats, dogs, and other creatures under her care. I got along with most of the animals, apart from *the birds*. Not to be disrespectful to Mama, but I hated those birds.

One of her birds was a myna bird. This bird, much like a parrot, would mimic what he heard. This was the bird I hated most of all. He was mean! Whenever Fran or I tried to clean his cage, he would bite us. I swear he thought we were his personal snack. He loved Mama though. On numerous occasions, I watched him crawl up Mama's arm and kiss her on the cheek.

One day, while we were at school, Mama had gone to run some errands. When Mama got home, she found a young lady on the porch, bawling her eyes out. Mama walked up the porch steps and asked the lady what was wrong.

"I've been waiting here for 20 minutes. Every time I ring the doorbell the lady inside says, 'I'll be right there... just a minute.'"

"I'm sorry. That's my bird," Mama explained. "That's what I say whenever the doorbell rings. The bird is a mimic."

The lady was asking for charitable donations. Mama donated, of course. It was the least she could do after the trauma her bird had caused the poor woman. After many years, Mama gave the bird to the zoo, where I'm sure it lived a long and happy life... probably tormenting other women and young children.

# Special Delivery

I was still in high school when my brother, George, was drafted to serve in Vietnam. During the early stages of the war, most Americans who did not make it overseas to serve our country, offered their skills, time, and money to contribute to the war effort. I, personally, logged hundreds of hours volunteering at the first aid center near home. However, the largest, and most memorable, contribution I made resulted from a letter George had sent home to the family.

The letter started out with a few pleasantries and a reassurance that he was meeting loads of new and interesting people. Fran and I were reading the letter together and the part that struck us as bizarre was at the end. "P.S. Send the *Sears and Roebucks* catalogue. We need toilet paper." I was so confused by this last statement that I turned to Mama and asked what he meant by it. Her clarification nearly sent me spinning into another dimension.

"Well, they don't have toilet paper where they are. They use the catalogue pages to wipe themselves after they use the bathroom." To which Fran and I replied, in unison, and with heartfelt disgust, "Eeeeww!" The two of us decided that this was just not acceptable. We began to pool our babysitting money. Eventually, we came up with enough to purchase a package of 144 individually wrapped rolls of Scott toilet paper, which we promptly mailed overseas to George.

We knew that our gift had been a big hit, but we didn't know just how big it was until well after the war had ended. Years later, George informed us that receiving our package was like receiving mail-order popularity. After receiving our gift, it didn't take him long to realize what a rare opportunity he had right at his fingertips. He briefly considered his options, and before long he became a regular salesman. The toilet paper rolls were hot commodities and "a steal" at ten dollars per roll! Those who invested in this luxury, guarded their purchase in a variety of ways. Some men wrote all over the inner tubes of their roll to identify them. Others went as far as to sleep on them as if they were pillows.

In the end, he sold every single roll, not even saving one roll for himself, and he made $1440. After selling the last roll, he sent home $1000 with a note asking Mama to, "Split the money between Evelyn and Fran's savings accounts." He kept the other $440 for himself.

# Civil Unrest

In April 1968, a classmate invited Fran and me to hear a preacher speak at a nearby Southern Baptist church. My classmate had heard he was "really good" but that's all she knew. Mama was open to having us explore other religions, so she agreed to let us go. I will never forget that preacher who stood at the pulpit and declared, with such conviction, that, "It doesn't matter what rocks are thrown at you in this world. It doesn't matter what people say to you. What matters is how you react to these things as they happen. God doesn't look at what is done to you, but what you do in response." The preacher was Martin Luther King Jr., he was killed a few days later.

I was 14 when King was assassinated. I was attending Sacred Heart Catholic School for girls in Memphis. King was in town aiding in the garbage collectors' strike. In the 1960s, garbage collectors were mainly black men. The white owners of Waste Management drastically underpaid these black workers. The purpose of the strike was to ensure these workers received a decent wage, better safety standards, and recognition of their union.

The Wednesday after his arrival, King led a march in downtown Memphis. He insisted that their demonstration be a peaceful one. Men linked arms, walked down the streets forming human chains, and protested discrimination. The protestors attempted to remain peaceful but, around one o'clock in the afternoon, policemen instigated the riots by showering the crowd with pellet gunfire and forceful torrents of water expelled from hoses.

I was at school, less than four miles away, when the riots began. I could hear the screaming from the crowds and smell the smoke from the gunfire. A few moments later our principal, Sister Pauline, came over the intercom and stated in rushed authority; "Classes will be canceled for the rest of the day. You will leave school now and you will go straight home. You will *NOT* go to get Krystal hamburgers. You will *NOT* go to Sears. You will *NOT* go to your friend's house. Again, you will go straight home. You will call us when you get home. We will call you back to make sure you're there. If you do not go straight home, you will be grounded until you graduate from college!"

We were naive enough to believe that she *could* ground us if she wanted to, so we all took her warnings seriously. Including Fran and myself, there were nine girls who rode the number 56 bus to school every day. We obediently walked straight to the bus stop. Little did we know the buses had stopped running several hours earlier.

About an hour after we left school, a large black lady in a white Cadillac pulled up in front of us and got out. She glared at us; her eyes filled with shock and concern. She hollered, "What are you girls doing? Don't you know there are riots going on out here?!" We were already so scared because we knew that Sister Pauline was going to have our butts on a platter, so we found it difficult to answer her. It didn't matter anyway. Without hesitation, she walked around the car toward us and began mumbling under her breath while she pitched us one by one into the backseat of her car. "... Stupid kids... don't have brains to pound sand in a rat hole... standing out here on the street... could get themselves killed..." After we were all loaded, she climbed back behind the wheel.

She drove each of us home, taking time to walk us to our front doors. Since Fran and I lived the farthest out, we were the last to be dropped off. By the time we arrived home it was 3:45 pm. The black lady escorted us to our door, holding our wrists as if we were rag dolls. I knew instantly that we were in trouble when I saw Mama standing in the doorway as we made our way up the walk. Mama was *never* late for work, and she was supposed to start that day at 2:30 pm. Apparently, Sister Pauline had called several times to see if we had arrived home safely. From the look on Mama's face, I couldn't tell if she was more worried or furious.

Before Mama could speak, the lady rattled off the monologue that she had spoken seven times that afternoon. "Don't get mad at them. They told me that they weren't supposed to get into cars with strangers. But I wasn't about to have them wait on a corner for a bus that would never come." Mama's expression softened as she fought to find words to relay her gratitude. The kind stranger spoke again quickly, "Don't say anything. I just hope you'd do the same for my children." With that, she walked away. We never even knew her name. After Mama knew that we were safe, she was determined to get to work. My brother Saro drove her straight to the hospital. We didn't know then that we wouldn't see Mama again for several days.

As a direct result of the riots, and King's assassination the next day, the city went into complete lockdown. Mama and all the hospital staff members were forced to remain at work, sleeping in the spare hospital wards. All the schools were shut down too. The entire city population was instructed to remain at home or in their place of business until further notice. The riots lasted for roughly four days.

When the chaos began dwindling down, Saro risked taking my siblings and me to McDonald's for lunch. While we were eating, a large tank pulled up at the drive-thru window. A man stuck his head out of the vehicle and began shouting his order in a deep southern drawl, "I'll take 16 cheeseburgers, 10 malts- make some of 'em chocolate, 11 orders of fries..." It was an amusing sight, but a humbling reminder of the tension the city was under, which would persist for many months.

# Lost in Translation

As a high school student, I enjoyed most of my classes. The class I loathed without shame was - *SPANISH*. I knew the importance of learning another language, of gaining a rounded global understanding... blah blah blah... but I just couldn't comprehend any of it. No matter how hard I studied, I just could not understand the material. The highest grade I could achieve was a D. In Catholic School, this was NOT acceptable. The nuns made their disappointment abundantly clear. My Spanish teacher, Sister Isabella, pointed out, "Your problem, Evelyn, is that you *think* in English and try to translate into Spanish when you really need to *think* in Spanish." Huh- well, that clears it up. It was no wonder that I failed and had to repeat the class.

At the completion of my second time through Spanish class, Sister Isabella knew I'd be repeating the course the following year... again. So, she gave me an assignment to advance my skills over the summer. She instructed me to translate the book of *Don Quixote*, in its entirety, into Spanish. I thought she was nuts, since that novel is over 900 pages long! Every day for three months I spent hours in my room pouring over the material, fuming with resentment at the inhumanity of depriving me of a summer vacation. I had no free time for anything. However, days before the end of summer, I finally completed the task and put down my pen with a sense of pride and accomplishment.

On the first day back to school, I walked into my Spanish class and dropped the completed translation on Sister Isabella's desk.

"There!" I exclaimed.

She looked at the pile of papers with obvious confusion, "What's this?"

"*Don Quixote.* Remember? You told me to translate it into Spanish over the summer?" I asked.

Her eyes grew wide, then she cleared her throat, and stammered, "Oh yeah, and I'm very glad you did it!"

She didn't fool me one bit. I couldn't believe it. I wasted my whole summer, and she did not even remember giving me this assignment. At that moment, I began wondering if it was possible to kill a nun and get away with it.

Since this was my third year of taking the same Spanish class, I'm happy to say that I did manage to achieve a C. A fat lot of good it did me though; to this day, I still only remember about three words in Spanish.

# Photos
# 1950s to 1960s

*Daddy, Mama, and me (1953)*

*Me (as the Nanook of the North)*
*and Daddy (1955)*

*Juanita riding on the Sluppick's Garage float in a town parade (1955)*

*Daddy and Me by his Company truck (1956)*

*Me- 4.5 years old, Fran- 3 years old (1958)*

*Our Little Army (1958). Left to Right: Florence (Mama), Frances, Evelyn (Me), Juanita, Mike, George Jr, Saro*

*Sluppick Family (1958). Back Row: Mike, George, Juanita, Saro, George (Daddy), Florence (Mama). Front Row: Frances, Evelyn (Me)*

*Grandma Evelyn Sluppick and Daddy (circa 1959)*

*Daddy after first stroke (circa 1960)*

# 1970s-1980s

# A Knight in Shining Armor

I was only ten years old when Daddy died. His death forced my siblings and me to grow up at an accelerated rate. Since we were the youngest, Fran and I were probably the most affected by this change.

Compared to most of the girls I knew, I had a much more rigorous schedule. After school, many of my girlfriends would go to the local Krystal hamburger joint but I spent my afternoons helping Mama around the house. I rarely went to parties or to school dances. When I was not doing housework or homework, I spent my free time reading books. During the summertime, I would get a job at an ice cream shop or bakery near my home. I never bothered with makeup or keeping up with the current fashion trends. I never considered myself unattractive, but I also knew that I wasn't extremely "girly."

When I was 18, my perspective on life changed. One day, in late November, I was set up on a blind date. I had never been on a blind date before, so I was both nervous and excited. I had spent a great deal of time primping and preparing. When my date came to the door, I walked downstairs to meet him. As I opened the door, I felt confident that my "day of beauty" had paid off. Unfortunately, that confidence shattered when the man in the doorway took one look at me and said with disgust, "I'm not that desperate," then walked away. I cannot say how long I stood there before I mustered enough energy to shut the door and return to my bedroom. I was devastated. My whole world seemed to crash and burn right before my eyes. I was living in a dorm at my nursing school. For the rest of the night, my roommate and I sat in our room watching sappy movies and commiserating over our lack of a love life.

The next day, Sergeant Morris, an officer in the United States Marine Corps, came to the nursing school dorm. He informed the House Mother that there was going to be a party for the graduating class of his unit, and he wanted to extend an invitation to the girls in my school. Considering the events from the previous night, I wasn't in the mood to go. I was persuaded to get out and have some fun. I got ready with less enthusiasm. I ended up tagging along with three of my classmates. That evening, Sergeant Morris came to pick us up. My classmates and I piled into his car with him and another soldier. Little did we know what we had gotten ourselves into.

When we entered the room where the party was being held, I knew something was a little odd. After a few general glances around, I figured out what it was. The room contained wall-to-wall Marines, but my friends and I were the only girls there! I became somewhat uneasy with this realization. However, I found myself particularly taken by the blue-eyed soldier who had ridden in with us, but I didn't know how to talk to him, and I wasn't any good at making the first move. When Sergeant Morris came to our table, I took a deep breath and seized my chance. I looked at him and whispered, "Who is that guy who drove in with us? He's kind of cute." Without even a slight hesitation he screamed across the room, "HEY DAVE! SOMEONE HERE IS HOT FOR YOUR BOD!" Was it my imagination, or did the room grow eerily quiet at that exact moment?

Luckily, Dave had a sense of humor, and he quickly relieved my embarrassment. We spent the rest of the night together just talking and laughing. It turned out that Dave had graduated a few years earlier and had come to the party just for the free food and beer. *How lucky was I?*

By the time Dave took me back to school, I felt like I was walking on clouds. We stood at my door, saying our goodbyes and telling each other what a great time we had, when he unexpectedly seized me in a full body embrace and proceeded to kiss me. I was shocked and didn't know how to react. After a few moments, which seemed like hours, I was ripped out of my momentary stupor when he proclaimed that he loved me.

I rewarded his sentiment the way any self-respecting woman would have done. I slapped him! "You don't love me," I yelled at him "You just met me." Then I ran inside, slamming the door behind me. I couldn't believe my bad luck. First the blind date, and now *this*? It didn't seem possible, but I was even more depressed than I had been the night before. I drowned my sorrows in a gallon of ice cream before turning in for the night.

At 6 a.m. the next morning, the House Mother came into my room to inform me that a young man in a suit was downstairs waiting to speak with me. For a moment I was paralyzed with fear.

I was sure that it was one of my brothers coming to get me because something had happened to Mama. When the feeling returned to my legs, I jumped out of bed. I just threw on whatever clothes were within my reach. The result was a pair of sweatpants, an old T-shirt, and a pair of mismatched socks, most of which were retrieved from the floor and could just as easily have been my roommate's. When I ran down the stairs, I came face to face with Dave.

"Hi," I stammered, "What are you doing here?"

"Well, it's Sunday. I figured I could take you to church." he replied matter-of-factly.

"Sure," I said with obvious confusion, "let me just go up and change." As I walked back upstairs, I noticed that my heart was racing a mile a minute.

That day, I knew Dave was different from any other man I'd ever known. We shared a beautiful day together and a few short weeks later we were engaged to be married. I have never regretted any part of my life with Dave. I thank God every day for that seemingly insignificant graduation party at which He brought us together.

# A Walk in the Park

I fell in love with Dave within a few weeks of getting to know him. I would go anywhere with him or do anything for him. If he had asked me to dive headfirst into a tank full of crocodiles, I would have rejoiced at the chance to be eaten alive. After Dave and I had been dating for a couple of months, he arrived at my nursing school one night and asked if I wanted to take a little romantic walk with him the next morning. Too easy- I was quick to comply.

That Sunday morning, I got dressed feeling the excitement of someone who had finally made it to the Olympics. Dave picked me up and we were on our way to what I expected to be a romantic stroll, alone with the man I loved. Imagine my surprise when we arrived at what appeared to *be* the Olympics! Dave had failed to mention that this "little walk" was, in fact, a 20-mile charity hike for the March of Dimes. Now, I am not completely without heart. I supported the March of Dimes, but I am not sure that I was ever prepared to walk 20 miles for the cause. Dave could tell I was reluctant. He told me that he was required to make the trek... for something to do with the Marine Corps... and he wanted my company. When he put it like that, I could hardly resist. Anyway, I was already there, what could it hurt? Turns out, it could hurt every inch of my entire body.

After the first few miles, I was already beginning to get sore. I told myself that I had to finish the walk for Dave. I gave myself mini goals as we walked.

"Just cross that road a few blocks ahead."

"Just make it to that streetlamp a few feet ahead."

And eventually, "Just put one foot in front of the other."

The last several miles of the hike were a blur. I felt like I was alone in the world, consumed by my aches and pains. I don't remember crossing the finish line, but I know I managed to stick it out for the whole 20 miles. By the end I was extremely sore, and I said to Dave in quiet desperation, "Don't make me walk anymore." He took me to the car where I instantly collapsed, and he went to get our certificates of completion. I rested in the car while Dave stood in a line that seemed to go on for miles itself. As I dosed off, I remember thinking what a strong man he was. I was not sure if Superman himself would have still been able to function after such a grueling event. Once he had collected whatever papers he was waiting for, he drove me back to my dorm.

Back at home, we sat on the couch in the common area and enjoyed each other's quiet company. Then I decided that I needed to see the written proof of my experience and I finally said, "Okay, let me see my certificate." Dave got stone-faced and it gave me a chill. After a moment he softened and casually asked me, "Didn't you get it?"

I was furious. *When was I supposed to have gotten it?* Turns out he was more like Clark Kent masquerading as Superman than the other way around. He stammered, "I'm sorry. I had just walked 20 miles. I wasn't thinking clearly. I might have forgotten to get my own certificate if I didn't need to show proof that I completed the walk to my commanding officer."

When I woke up to get ready for classes the next morning, I could barely move. I started to get up to walk to the bathroom, but I fell flat on my face. My stiffness and soreness persisted throughout the following week. It was probably a good thing that Dave maintained his distance until I recovered. After that I was a bit more cautious when Dave suggested a romantic outing. In retrospect, I am quite proud that I completed the entire walk. I just wish I had proof in writing.

# Against My Mother's Wishes

I was 18 when I met Dave on November 22, 1971. We had what some people might classify as a whirlwind courtship. We had only been dating a month as Christmas drew nearer. I really had no idea what my Christmas gift from him was going to be. My roommate, on the other hand, thought she knew exactly what he was planning. She was certain, beyond the shadow of a doubt, that he was intending to propose. Dave and I had briefly discussed marriage a couple of weeks earlier, but I doubted the possibility that it would happen so soon. After a few days, I had convinced myself that my roommate was right, and I knew instantly that my answer would be "yes." I anxiously waited for the day that he would choose to ask for my hand in marriage.

On Christmas Eve, Dave picked me up and told me that we were going to Sears and Roebuck so we could get my gift. As we walked through the department store, my heart was nearly jumping out of my chest. We approached the jewelry section—- and then walked right past it. My eyes stared longingly at the rings, while my body reluctantly followed Dave. My heart sunk deep into my stomach as I realized that I was *not* getting a proposal that day. I had spent so much energy believing that I would be receiving a ring that I hadn't really considered what else my surprise could be. Finally, Dave came to a halt... in the toy department.

"Pick anything you want," Dave said with glee, certain that the shocked look on my face was because he had found the perfect gift. Feeling betrayed and disappointed, I looked around at all the stuffed animals and other toys. After a few minutes I picked up a little stuffed lion whose head turned clockwise to a musical tune.

A month later, on January 22, 1972, Dave and I were on a bus heading for home. It was around 11 o'clock at night and we were involved in a relatively minor argument. It started when Dave announced that he wanted *ten* children.

"Not unless *you're* planning to deliver nine of them," I declared firmly.

"Don't you want to have my children?" He asked.

"No, not really," I told him nonchalantly.

"What?" Dave responded, looking a bit hurt.

"Well, I'm not Henry Ford. I don't need to pop out a new model every year!" I told him.

Our argument got a bit heated, but we didn't realize how loud we had gotten until the driver kicked us off the bus. Undaunted, we continued to argue as we walked the remaining three miles home.

Finally, Dave shouted, "ISN'T IT ENOUGH THAT I WANT *YOU* TO HAVE MY KIDS?"

"Yes!" I shouted back at him. Then we walked on in silence.

After a few moments he asked, "Did I just propose to you?"

"Yes, and you can't take it back," I answered. We walked the rest of the way home holding hands and wearing smiles on our faces.

Unfortunately, just agreeing to get married wasn't enough to guarantee an easy road to the altar. First, we had to break the news to Mama. She was against it from the start. Mama believed that I was too young to get married and desperately wanted me to refuse the proposal. Even though I was sure I would marry Dave, I did consider Mama's objections because I valued her opinion greatly.

I was close to giving in to Mama when Dave dropped a bomb a few days later. We were on a date when he stated with urgency, "Evelyn, I'm being transferred to California."

Oblivious of the significance of what he was telling me, I replied, "When are you going to be back?"

"No, Evelyn, I'm being *transferred*, as in *I'm not coming back.*"

I loved Dave, and I couldn't picture my future without him. I realized, then and there, that I had a decision to make. Should I marry Dave despite my mother's objections, or to be an obedient daughter and call off our engagement? Quickly, I realized that there was nothing to consider. I was destined to be Dave's wife.

When we broke the news to Dave's family, they were thrilled. They even insisted that we accelerate the wedding plans. *My* entire family, however, still wholeheartedly opposed the wedding. Mama and I fought endlessly over my engagement, but I continued to make the preparations. When it came time to set the exact date, I had no doubt in my mind that we should be married on June 17$^{th}$, because that's my parents' anniversary. Since Daddy couldn't be at my wedding, I figured this would be the best way to honor him.

Mama wasn't as keen on the idea. "That is *my* anniversary, you get *your own* anniversary," she told me furiously.

I refused to argue over another issue surrounding my wedding; so, Dave and I chose to be married the following weekend on June 24th. Three weeks before our wedding, in a last-ditch effort to get me to cancel the ceremony, Mama started chasing me around the house. Agreeing to marry Dave was the first thing I ever did against my mother's wishes, but I wasn't prepared to change my mind.

Finally, she stopped mid-run and demanded to know, "What would be the worst thing that could happen if you didn't marry Dave?!"

I looked her straight in the eyes and replied, "The worst thing that could happen is that I wouldn't be married to him."

"I don't understand." Mama stated, with exasperated frustration.

"I would have to know that he was somewhere in the world, and I wasn't his wife. I'm going to marry him, Mama. If you want to be there, fine. If you don't want to be there then that's okay too." I said without flinching. Mama still didn't consent to our marriage, but she no longer tried to dissuade me against it either.

As years went by, Mama became less resistant toward Dave. However, it wasn't until she'd suffered a stroke that I fully believed that she had accepted my marriage. I was kneeling at her side, as she lay in bed slipping away from this world, when suddenly she reached out and took my hand in hers. She looked directly into my eyes, with her eyes drowning in emotion, and said, "You and Dave have been married longer than your father and I was." To an outsider, it wouldn't seem like much, but to me those thirteen little words spoke volumes.

# A Right Arm to the Rescue

Dave was stationed in Memphis while awaiting his final orders to be transferred to El Toro Marine Base in California. After we had been engaged for about four months, Dave received a weekend pass that allowed us to go to Piqua, Ohio, to spend his birthday with his family. On the drive to Ohio, we made a pit stop in Louisville, Kentucky, to visit Dave's best man. By the time we left Kentucky, it had begun to rain. I wasn't concerned because Dave was an excellent driver.

Not long into the drive, we encountered something on the road. The rain had blocked the obstruction from view until we were almost on top of it. It was the dead body of a large dog. Although he tried, Dave couldn't avoid hitting it. Preparing himself for impact, he braced himself as far back into the seat as he could with his hands clutching hard to the steering wheel. Right before we collided with the dead animal, Dave had managed to extend his right arm across my chest to secure me against my seat. Then, suddenly, Dave pulled me down so that my face was parallel to my knees and laid his body on top of mine. We remained in this position as our

Opel Kaddett continued to flip end over end, a total of seven times. The action of holding me down caused him to dislocate both of his shoulders. We had a little portable radio in the backseat of the car. During the ordeal, the radio had flown forward and hit me in the back of the head causing several blood vessels in my head to burst. My entire face was blood-red, and my eyes felt like they were bulging out of their sockets.

I must have blacked out after that because the next thing I remember is lying face-up on the ground staring into the face of a large man who appeared to be hovering right above me. He kept repeating, in a reassuring voice, "Everything is going to be fine." After a moment, my head cleared, and I remembered Dave. I began frantically asking about him, but I received the same response repeatedly. "He's okay. He's going to be okay." That wasn't enough. I desperately wanted him next to me so I could find out for myself. Then, out of the corner of my eye, I saw the hearse. I was sure that he was dead, and I started to cry. I learned later that, in this small town just outside of Louisville, the town hearse *doubled* as the town ambulance.

The medics tried to take Dave to the hospital right away, but he refused to go until I was ready to go as well. The next thing I remember was being taken to a hospital in Cincinnati, Ohio. By the time we arrived, my face had swollen to twice its normal size and bruises had appeared on my chest from Dave pushing me against the seat. I needed immediate medical attention, but the hospital refused to treat me without consent from my next of kin. During the accident, my engagement ring had turned around on my finger so that the only part showing was the gold band. Dave took this to his advantage and told the doctors that he and I were just married.

“Where’s the marriage license?” the head doctor asked with a smirk.

Dave unflinching answered, “It’s in the car. Good luck trying to find it.”

They finally took care of me under Dave’s proviso.

While I was in the hospital, I drifted in and out of consciousness. In one of my clear moments, I vividly remember Dave coming into my room. Hardly able to look at him, I stuttered between sobs, “I’m so ugly, I suppose you won’t want to marry me now.” Dave met my eyes and said with love in his voice, “You have never been more beautiful to me.”

When we were released from the hospital, Dave’s mother and sister-in-law came to pick us up. His mother burst into tears the moment she saw us and, even though we were standing right in front of her, it took some doing for Dave to convince her that we were not dead. Once we were back in Piqua, we had the daunting task of contacting the highway patrol to see if anything could be salvaged from the wreck. There was one item that I was sure we’d never see again. It was a coffee can that we used to keep our spare change in; the spare change we used for emergencies.

As expected, we were informed that the car had been totaled. In fact, we were horrified to discover that the roof of our vehicle had been crushed down so that it was level with the hood and trunk. Among the things that managed to survive the crash were the four brand new tires we had just put on the car. Amazingly, we received most of our belongings back, including, to our surprise, the coffee can. We learned that, at the time of our accident, the car directly behind us contained four medical students from the University of Cincinnati. They had been listening to the radio play,

"Every time it rains, it rains pennies from heaven," when the coffee can hit their windshield and showered loose change over the front end of their vehicle. With a glimmer of hope, I opened the canister to see if any of our small change had survived the crash. As expected, our collection of change must have been scattered on the freeway. However, the can was not empty. Our coins had been replaced with five-dollar and ten-dollar bills.

With our newfound wealth, Dave was able to buy airline tickets for us to fly back to Memphis. Mama picked us up at the airport and gave us a thorough once-over as well. She was most relieved that, even though my face was red and swollen, my eyes were untouched by our recent tragedy. I have no doubt that my trendy goggle-style glasses saved my eyes from any permanent damage.

This near-death experience reminded me of how precious and fragile life is, and how important it is for us to live, love, and be in the moment. I know that, for most people, a near-death experience is usually defined as "having been pronounced dead but then returning to life." However, I believe a near-death experience can also be defined as "a situation where someone should have died in some event and, by some miracle, was pulled from the fingers of death and allowed to live on." There is no other explanation as to how we survived a collision of that magnitude. For all intents and purposes, we should *not* have walked away from that crash, but I am so grateful that we did.

# Newlyweds

Shortly after our wedding, I became pregnant. A few months later, Dave was sent on a temporary assignment to Washington State. While he was there, I lived with my mother-in-law in Ohio. By the time Dave came back to take me with him to California, I was six months pregnant with our first child. It was the middle of February, and we decided to drive across the country to our new home. We loaded the car with most of our belongings. The mattress was too big to fit in the trunk, so we tied it to the roof of the car. Then we were on our way. Dave was going to do the driving while I navigated. A few days into the journey, I was looking at the map trying to figure out if we should go north or south of the Colorado Mountains. I pointed Dave, in what I thought was, the right direction. Unfortunately, we had driven about 500 miles before we realized that I was holding the map upside down. By that time, it was so late that we opted to just call it a night.

We walked into the lobby of the first motel we came across and quickly discovered that we were in for an adventure. The clerk greeted us, stating in a less-than-enthusiastic tone, "Okay. The room has two beds in it. It'll be $6 if you use one bed and make it, $8 if you use one bed and don't make it, $10 if you use two beds and make them, and $12 if you use two beds and don't make them." We were so afraid to sleep under the covers because we had no idea when, or if, the sheets had ever been changed.

The next day we left early so that we'd arrive in California by nightfall. As we made our way through Colorado, we were caught in a horrible rainstorm with blustering winds. By the time we completed our trek to the west coast, our mattress had frozen at a 90-degree angle. For a month, we slept on the floor until our mattress defrosted enough to be usable.

For the first six years of our marriage, I was the happiest woman on the planet. I was content with being Dave's wife and staying at home to take care of our girls. In 1978, however, shortly after Margaret was born, I began to get restless. When I agreed to marry Dave, I opted to give up nursing school to relocate to California and become a stay-at-home Mom. As much as I loved being a wife and a mother, I felt the growing need to go back. After thinking it over, I decided to discuss it with Dave. We talked about it for a few days, but nothing really came out of it.

Then one day, early in December, I came home from running errands and I found a large pile of wrapped boxes in the living room.

"What's this?" I asked Dave.

"It's an early Christmas," he answered with a smile.

I discovered that all the packages were mine, so I sat down and excitedly started opening the gifts. To my surprise, I unwrapped several nursing school textbooks and in one of the books

I discovered a completed school registration form. With Dave's love and support, I went back to school the following semester. After a few years, I completed my certification as a Registered Nurse (RN). I worked as an RN for several years while I continued my education. I eventually received a degree as a Certified Rehabilitation Registered Nurse. I will always treasure my profession. Not only was it a rewarding career path but it provided me with an additional connection to Mama who practiced nursing until she died.

# Student Driver on Board

For many American teenagers, turning 16 years old is synonymous with obtaining a driver's license and gaining some control over one's own schedule. My 16th birthday didn't come with that ticket to freedom. For me, knowing how to drive was unnecessary. Everywhere I needed to go was either in walking distance or a short bus ride away. Honestly, I had no interest in getting behind the wheel. It wasn't until I met Dave that I really thought much about driving at all.

A few months after we met, we were in his car and Dave suggested that I should drive him to work so I could use the car for the day. "I don't know how to drive," I told him. I am surprised he didn't run off the road from shock. "How can you live in America and not know how to drive?" He asked disbelievingly. "I don't need to drive since Memphis has a great public transportation system," I responded.

For Dave, driving was a big part of life. He grew up in a small town and had been driving since he was about 13 years old when a local merchant asked for his help making deliveries. True, he didn't get officially licensed until well after he turned 16 but, none-the-less, he had the experience. So, Dave made it his mission to teach me how to drive.

For weeks, I studied the rules and regulations of the road. When he felt I was ready to take the test, we were visiting his family in Ohio. He told me, "I'll take you for the test when we get back to Memphis because you'll never pass the driving test in Ohio." I was insulted. Then he explained that the driving test in his small town was extremely tough, and they tested every possible scenario. He added, "They will even make you parallel park." He figured the test in my larger town might be more lenient. Boy, was that an understatement.

When we got back to Memphis, he drove me to the police station where the tests were administered. Once we checked in, the officer walked me out to our car and instructed me to drive around the block. He opened the driver's side door, and I got in. When he closed the door he said, "Okay see you when you get back." Dave asked in astonishment, "Wait, aren't you going to get in the car with her?" The officer responded, "She doesn't have a license! She could kill me! If she gets back in one piece and we don't hear any crashing, then, I figure, she can drive." Somehow, I made it back and finally got my driver's license.

Even though I had my license, I didn't expect to use it much. Dave was always around if I needed to go somewhere and I preferred to be the passenger. Dave and I were married, and I became pregnant with Jessica. Dave was preparing for his transfer to California when he received his orders to go overseas to fight in the Vietnam War. I was scared on so many levels. Not the least of which knowing that I'd have to drive the freeway to get to my doctor's appointments. I had never driven the freeway, so Dave insisted I start practicing. I was stubborn and I refused.

One day he was driving me to an appointment and, without warning, pulled the car to the side of the freeway and got out. "What are you doing?" I asked in disbelief. He opened my car door and said, "Evelyn, I am going to war, and I won't be here to drive you around. So, if you want to get to your appointments, you need to learn to drive the freeway." I was scared and I protested, "Dave, I can't!" He just stood there, so I added, "We're going to be late." He stated matter-of-factly, "Well, then you better start driving." I reluctantly got behind the wheel. I cried and complained the whole way but managed to get us there safely. As it turned out, America pulled out of the war before Jessica was born. Dave's orders were canceled, and he wasn't sent to Vietnam. However, thanks to his persistence, I am now able to drive freeways without bursting into tears.

# Matters of the Mind

After high school, I decided to continue my education by going to nursing school. I wasn't majoring in psychology but courses in the subject were required. I will forever remember the Psychology professor who prided himself on never giving a perfect score on any assignment because, "there is no such thing as a perfect paper." The final paper had to be 26 pages long, typed, and single spaced! The topic could be anything we wanted if it was preapproved by him. I wanted to impress him. I asked, "Can I write on the physiological and psychological ramifications of having a mastectomy?" He said, "You can try, but I don't think you'll get much out of it. There isn't much research on the topic." I looked forward to the challenge.

Throughout the course, I worked diligently on my final paper. We didn't have the luxury of a word processor or computer. I would type, proofread, and retype each page until I was satisfied with the result, and then move onto the next page. I meticulously reviewed my work because I was determined to hand in an assignment as close to perfect as possible.

After several weeks of this routine, I had completed 24 pages which were resting in the chair next to me. I was busy working on page 25 when, to my dismay, Mama walked in and promptly sat on top of my completed pages. I was mortified. I had to retype the entire paper because I was not about to get docked points for turning in a crinkly essay.

I managed to get the assignment finished on time with the confidence that I had done a thorough job. I knew the professor thought so too because, when I got my paper back, a big 98 beamed back at me from the top of my first page. After class, my professor pulled me aside and asked permission to make a copy for himself. I responded, "Sure. Can I ask why?" He said, "I have a wife and three daughters, and I want them each to read your report."

In another one of my Psychology courses my professor wanted to teach us the importance of following directions. For the last six weeks of class, we sat and listened to our professor emphasizing this point. The last week of class was the most crucial. On Monday we discussed the final, on Wednesday the final was administered, and on Friday we got the results.

During the Monday discussion, we were informed that without a passing grade on the final, we were guaranteed not to get an A in the class. No late arrivals would be permitted to participate. If we left to go to the bathroom, the doors would lock behind us. We could bring nothing with us to the exam except for a single pen.

When I entered the auditorium on Wednesday, butterflies flooded my stomach. The room was packed with 350 students. The desks were divided by wooden boards and on top of each desk was a mound of paper facing down. At the start of the exam, we were informed the test contained 600 questions and we had three hours to complete them.

I read the first question; *Read every single question on this test and then answer them. Can you follow directions?"* I nearly panicked. How could they expect us to read all the questions before answering any of them?! However, thanks to my years at Catholic School, I was conditioned to read the last question first on any test I took. Boy, was I glad I did. As I flipped to the last question I stared in disbelief.

*Do not answer any questions on this test. Did you follow directions?*

For a moment I thought there was no way this professor could be that mean but, nonetheless, I put my pen under my knee to prevent myself from answering any of the questions. For about two hours and forty-five minutes, I sat twiddling my thumbs while reading through the test packet. I knew when the three hours were coming to an end when, suddenly, I heard hundreds of students desperately trying to erase pen ink.

On Friday my professor called six students, including me, to the front of the class. I thought, *Great- Not only did I fail, but I'm failing in public.* However, once to the front, it was revealed that we were the only six that passed the test. He asked each of us how we did it.

Two had started reading the packet and never got through all the questions. Two others, like me, read the last question first. The last guy said he read the first question and thought, "screw this" and refused to do any of it.

The funniest part of the whole thing is that the questions were exceedingly stupid. One question was, "How do you spell the numeral 2?" To which he was receiving answers like "TO," "TOO," "TWO," or "THE NUMERAL TWO." Another question asked, "Can a man marry his widow's sister?" To which one guy replied, "Why not? This is America, isn't it?" *Hello- if he has a widow, he's dead*! So, essentially, when all was said and done, I managed to pass the biggest idiot test of all time.

A short time after completing my training to be a Licensed Vocational Nurse (LVN), I decided to go back to school to complete my training as a Registered Nurse (RN). One of the first and most memorable courses I took was another in psychology.

On the first day of class, we were given an assignment that was to be turned in at the end of the semester. The professor passed a bowl around the class containing small pieces of folded paper. Each paper had an assignment on it and no two were alike.

Just after the bowl made its way around the room, I noticed a guy a few rows behind me glancing my way and smiling. I had noticed him earlier and he seemed nice, so I smiled back. After class, while I was walking out of the door, this guy bumped into me. I thought nothing about it. I just said, "Excuse me," and kept walking.

After a few seconds I noticed that he was following me. He was just close enough that I could hear him humming. After a few minutes I started walking faster. He matched my pace. By the time I had reached my car I dropped everything I was carrying as I tried desperately to unlock the door. I was in tears when he walked up behind me and said, "Evelyn."

I almost peed my pants as I spun around and begged, "Please don't hurt me!"

He calmly stated, “Evelyn, it’s my assignment. Here, look.” He handed me the little piece of paper with his assignment written on it. *Intimidate Someone.* Even though it was a semester project, he turned in his paper the next day. I wasn’t happy to be his guinea pig and, from that day forward, I no longer thought he was a nice guy, and I didn’t like him one tiny iota.

# Knowledge is Power

After Dave was transferred to California, we lived in base housing at El Toro Marine Base. One day, I was in my living room with Jessica who was a year old. A good friend of mine, another military wife, was sitting in the chair next to me, listening as I read the comics to Jessica.

"Ah wish ah could do that," she suddenly said.

"Do what?" I asked.

"Ah wish ah could read the comics."

"Here," I said, as I handed her the page of comics that I had just finished.

"No, ah can't read." she stated matter-of-factly.

I looked at her in shock. I couldn't understand how someone could not have learned to read. I offered to teach her. She accepted but asked that I not tell her husband so she could surprise him. For a few months I ransacked Jessica's bookcases and grabbed every book from the *Sesame Street Alphabet* to *See Jane Run*. I would sit with my friend for hours teaching her the alphabet. Then the day came when she wanted to share her secret with her husband. We went down to the base store and purchased some food for dinner. Then, we went back to her house to prepare it. My friend invited Dave and I to supper. When it came time to eat, she placed the meal in front of us. Her husband looked at the meat that he knew had not been in the freezer.

"Where'd you get this?" He asked.

"Ah bought it."

"How?"

"Ah went ta the store an' ah read the sign. Ah read 'Chuck Roast' an' ah bought it."

"Where'd you learn to read?" He questioned.

"Evelyn taught me."

Her husband looked at me, then his hand rose, but before he could strike me Dave reached out and grabbed him by the wrist and growled, "Don't you dare lay a finger on my wife."

It was at that moment that I realized, her husband wanted her to be "stupid" so he could control her. Within a couple of years, their marriage ended in divorce. She wanted to continue her education, and she enrolled in the city college. The last I heard she had achieved a PhD. I guess the saying is true: "You are never too old to learn."

# A San Francisco Treat

I'll never forget the first time I visited San Francisco. Dave had a hankering to drive up the coast for a long weekend, and I couldn't resist. So, I loaded the car with an overnight bag and our daughter, Jessica. Jessica was 16 months old.

We arrived in San Francisco late on a Friday night. We were tired, hungry, and in search of a hotel. By the time we found a place to stay and unpacked, it was almost 1 AM on Saturday morning. Since we were still hungry, we went in search of anything that was open. We happened upon a little Italian restaurant.

This little restaurant was a classy joint. Unfortunately, there was no kid's menu. Dave and I didn't have a whole lot of money so we agreed that Jessica could just eat from our plates. I ordered lasagna and Dave ordered spaghetti and meatballs.

Due to the early hour, there weren't many patrons at the restaurant. In fact, other than us, there was only one large group in the back. I kept stealing glances at the group because one of the men looked familiar. After a short time, I realized why. It was

Burgess Meredith! I knew him best from his role in the Twilight Zone episode "Time Enough at Last" where an avid book lover finds himself alone with his books after a nuclear war. I badly wanted to say something, but I didn't want to make a scene. So, I wrote him a note on a napkin, which read, "Thank You. I have loved watching your work throughout the years. I hope you know, you bring joy to people's lives." I asked the waitress to see that he got the note. Dave asked why I didn't go over and get his autograph. I explained that he was eating dinner and that he deserved his privacy too.

A short time later, to our surprise, the actor approached our table, and Jessica turned on the charm like she was at an audition. She paraded up and down the booth in her white knit dress, flipping her stark white-blond hair. She had specks of spaghetti sauce on her cheeks that she wouldn't let me wipe off. Periodically she stopped long enough to pluck a meatball off Dave's spaghetti or to grab a handful of noodles, which she'd try to eat from the end with her arm stretched to its max.

Burgess Meredith addressed me first, "What's your business here?" I replied, "We had a long weekend and decided to get out for a little fun." Then he turned to Dave and said, "You're lucky to have this time to spend with your family. I wish I had taken a little time to travel with my children when they were young." He said it with such sincerity that I almost cried. We thanked him and he left to pay his bill.

We enjoyed the rest of our meal marveling over our celebrity encounter and his heartfelt words. We finished about a half an hour later and Dave went to get the bill while I waited in the booth with Jessica.

Dave returned and said in disbelief, “There’s no check. Apparently, Burgess Meredith covered our meal.” I was shocked, impressed, and humbled all at the same time. What a nice and gentle man. We left the restaurant feeling as though we’d encountered an angel walking among us.

# The Cost of a Lollipop

Jessica was about 18 months old when I found out that I was pregnant with Sarah. I was aware that a new baby would change our family dynamic, so I spent the following months talking to Jessica about the new addition to our family. I wanted to make the transition to a family of four as smooth as possible. Regardless of how much I prepared her, I wasn't sure how Jessica would react when Dave and I brought Sarah home from the hospital. As a last-ditch effort to soften the blow, we bought Jessica a life-like baby doll with three changeable outfits.

One month before I was due to deliver, Sarah insisted on entering the world early. I was desperately concerned about her timing because we simply were not ready. Sarah came home to an unfinished nursery and had nowhere to sleep. For the first few weeks, Dave and I made do by sharing our bed with her. Since our queen-sized four-poster bed stood at least two feet off the ground, I surrounded Sarah with every pillow I could find, to ensure her safety while she napped during the day.

About two weeks after we brought Sarah home from the hospital, Jessica showed us how much she loved her new baby sister. I was in the kitchen helping Dave get ready for work, when I heard Jessica calling me from the hall, "Mommy, Mommy." I looked over and saw Jessica with her baby doll. Turning to Dave, I whispered, "Oh, isn't that cute? Jessica put one of Sarah's dresses on her doll. I wonder how she got it?" Then, as if time stopped and I was standing in quicksand, I froze. It wasn't Sarah's dress on Jessica's baby doll. It was Sarah's dress on *SARAH*!

Jessica was not quite two years old, and I was afraid that she would drop the baby. So, I approached her with caution and asked, "Can we have the baby, please?" I tried using this tactic for the next few minutes, feeling as if I was trying to coax a criminal to let go of their hostage. Jessica wasn't hurting Sarah, but I was growing more nervous by the second. Then, Dave had the brilliant idea of trying to bribe Jessica. He grabbed a lollipop and attempted to convince her that she wanted the lollipop *more* than she wanted the baby. Finally, after what seemed like an eternity, she handed Sarah over and started munching on her prize.

After my panic subsided, I made my way to the bedroom, anxious to see what sort of mess was awaiting me. To my utter surprise, I walked into an unchanged scene. Since my bed was twice as tall as Jessica, I half expected to see some books or boxes propped up against the bed. Or, perhaps, the dresser drawers opened with the contents askew. Strangely, I didn't see anything that might look like a makeshift step stool. Stranger yet, was the condition of the bed itself. The blanket wasn't yanked down, the sheets were still in place, and *not one* of the pillows had been moved.

Dave and I still speculate on the circumstances surrounding that day, and we never figured out how Jessica managed to get Sarah out of that bed.

# All I Want for Christmas

As Dave and I continued our courtship, I grew to love everything about him. Well, almost everything. I wasn't a fan of his smoking habit. He wasn't a social smoker, a stress smoker, or even an after-dinner smoker. He was, in fact, a classic I-don't-have-to-have-a-reason-to-smoke chain smoker. On average, he went through about three packs a day. I never really tried to convince him to quit because I knew that, in the end, he would only stop if he truly wanted to.

In 1977, Dave was in his seventh year of service with the Marine Corps. His military commitment was ending, and he had decided that he did not wish to re-enlist for another term of service.

One day, in early October, he called me up while he was working on the base and asked me what I wanted for Christmas.

"I want you to quit smoking. Also, there's this book..." I responded nonchalantly.

"Okay," he replied.

"You'll give me the book?" I asked excitedly.

“No, I’ll quit smoking,”

I was skeptical because we had just purchased a carton of cigarettes a few days earlier. I had no reason to believe that he would honestly quit cold turkey, so I took that carton of cigarettes and stuck it in the freezer. They stayed there waiting for the day when Dave would throw in the towel and resort to old habits.

It was an odd sight to see Dave without a cigarette in his hand. It didn’t take long for people to notice that something was different when he walked into a room. When questioned by his peers, he casually informed them that he had decided to quit. Unfortunately, no one believed him. Generally, “quitting” implied that a person had quit *buying* cigarettes, not necessarily that they had quit *smoking* them. Dave’s friends and co-workers were constantly offering him cigarettes. To my surprise, even with this added pressure, Dave resisted the urge to light up.

When I was six months pregnant with Margaret, Dave and I were in a restaurant having lunch. At the time, all restaurants in California were still divided into smoking and non-smoking sections. To humor Dave’s insistence that he had quit for good, we requested a non-smoking booth. Luckily, our table was so deep into this section that we couldn’t even smell the smoke that drifted over from the smoking section. About halfway through our meal, a man sitting at a table next to us lit up a cigarette. Instead of blowing the smoke towards his dining companion, he politely turned his head and exhaled directly into my face. I immediately started to become nauseated. We asked the restaurant manager to address the situation, but he wasn’t willing to confront this individual and possibly cause a scene.

“We have to leave, I’m feeling sick.” I finally told Dave.

Instead of standing up and giving in to this man's inconsiderate behavior, Dave turned his head and looked at our neighbor. He stared at that man for a good five minutes before the stranger finally became irritated.

"What is your problem, buddy?" he demanded of Dave.

"I'm sorry but I've never seen one," Dave said with amazement.

"You've never seen what? A cigarette?"

"No, I've never seen a statistic," Dave replied with awe.

"Huh?"

"Someone who is functionally illiterate. Here, let me help you," Dave read as he pointed to the sign that was hanging less than ten feet away, "*Thank You for Not Smoking*." The man looked at Dave and then reluctantly put out his cigarette.

That was when I knew that Dave had officially quit smoking. When we arrived home that night, we took the carton of cigarettes out of the freezer. Dave took it to work the next day and gave the packs away to his friends. He has been smoke-free since October 1977.

# Security Blanket

When Sarah was little, she had two quirks that set her apart from my oldest. First, she could sleep anywhere. Rarely, however, did she sleep in her own bed. Dave and I took to leaving the hall light on at night, to avoid stepping on her when we woke to use the bathroom. Second, she loved my satin slips and undergarments. Many times, I found her rummaging through my dresser drawers to latch onto a nightgown so she could curl up and fall asleep. She never sucked her thumb. Instead, she would sleep while absentmindedly rubbing my slip, or what have you, between the fingers of her left hand and sucking the two middle fingers on her right. It was precious, but this habit of hers often left me frantically searching for clean under things.

I needed something innovative. I spent several weeks buying all the satin that I could find. I went to yard sales, church rummage sales, and thrift stores until I bought out every piece of satin clothing there was in the city. Then, I poured all my time into fashioning a cotton blanket with a three-inch satin trim around the outside. The day I finished the blanket was likely the happiest day in Sarah's life. This simple cloth never left Sarah's side. She carried it everywhere and my underwear thanked me. This was a beautiful arrangement.

When Sarah was about two-and-a-half years old, and I was pregnant with Margaret, I made a tragic mistake. I decided it was time to attempt washing this baby masterpiece. It was the middle of the day, and I was doing laundry when I realized that I couldn't locate Sarah. I looked for her in all the usual places. I figured she couldn't be far away, but I began to wonder if she might have gotten outside. I decided to start the load in the washer before I initiated a search of every room, closet, drawer, and crevice inside and around the house and yard. This proved to be a wise decision. Just as I was about to saturate my dirty clothes with liquid detergent, I looked down. I almost missed seeing the little body curled around the inside of the washer, clutching her blanket, and sucking her two middle fingers.

I never figured out how she managed to get in there, but I kept a close eye on her when I washed her blanket from that day forward. She eventually outgrew sucking her fingers, but she can still manage to sleep anywhere, and she never quite outgrew her love for soft, satiny things.

# I Am What I Am

By the time Sarah was walking and talking, Jessica was determined to establish her alpha role as older sister. Jessica picked on Sarah mercilessly and was always trying to get her into trouble. There were times that Sarah ended up with mysterious bumps and bruises, that I suspected were inflicted by Jessica, although neither would admit it, and they rarely fought in my presence. I figured this display of sibling rivalry was a natural part of childhood. I wanted my children to grow up into independent adults who could take care of themselves. I figured the best way to do this was to let them fight and solve their problems themselves with little or no intervention from Dave and me. This usually worked out okay, but sometimes I knew our intervention was necessary. One such time was when Sarah was about two years old.

One of their favorite cartoons at the time was *Popeye*. Jessica loved to play "Popeye" with Sarah. She would walk up to Sarah, claim she was Popeye who ate his spinach, and proceed to hit Sarah. If I witnessed this violence, I would punish Jessica, but I wasn't always in the room when it happened.

Finally, one day Sarah must've had enough of Jessica always beating up on her. I was in the kitchen when I heard the girls in the other room. Sarah said, "*This* time *I'm* Popeye and *you're* Brutus and I just ate *my* spinach." I entered the room just in time to see Sarah knock Jessica flat on the floor in one punch. I immediately rushed to Jessica to revive her. It took a few minutes for Jessica to come around but, luckily, she was fine. Jessica still picked on Sarah after that, but she never again played "Popeye."

# The Stork Strikes Again

I was pregnant with Jessica when Dave and I moved to California. One of our first tasks was to find an OBGYN to get me through the end of my pregnancy. We found Dr. Mike Akrawi. Dr. Akrawi had a rule that if the pregnant woman had a husband, then both parents were to be present at every prenatal appointment. When the doctor met me in the examination room for my first appointment, he asked where Dave was.

"He's in the waiting room." I answered.

"Excuse me," he said as he got up and walked out the door. As I sat there, I could hear him saying "Were you in the waiting room while she was getting pregnant?" They returned to the exam room together. I instantly liked him.

Dr. Akrawi had another rule that any person who was to be present at the birth must take classes to prepare. I was too far into my pregnancy and Dave didn't have enough time to attend these classes. It made me nervous that I might have to go through the experience alone. The doctor assured us that he could let this prerequisite slide. He told Dave, "You're a Marine, you can handle it." Dr. Akrawi delivered Jessica and, subsequently, Sarah.

My first two pregnancies went smoothly. I assumed my third would be smooth as well. From the moment I went into the Labor Room, things got chaotic. For starters, the wheels on my hospital bed wouldn't lock, so every time someone bumped into my bed, it would roll across the room. Early on, I was feeling enormous pressure in my gut which became more pronounced every time the bed rolled.

Dr. Akrawi came into the room in his Hawaiian shirt, obviously having been called in from a day off. I started begging him to allow me to have the bowel movement that was putting so much pressure on my gut. He complied and pulled out the bedpan only to discover that my bowels weren't causing the pressure. Startled, he announced, "That's no bowel movement, that's a baby! HOLD IT!" The doctor insisted we move to the Delivery Room immediately. As we were going through the door, the wheels of my bed finally decided to lock. The doctor was at my head while the nurse was at my business end. They tried to force the bed through, but it wouldn't budge, so, I said through gritted teeth, "Doctor if she delivers this baby, she's getting the fee!"

After a few moments of witnessing this struggle, Dave said, in his ever-tactful way, "F*** this," and he lifted my bed up and then pushed it, scraping the floor all the way to the delivery room. This was the first time Dave had brought a camera to snap pictures of the birth. When he wasn't pushing my bed with Hercules-like strength, he was taking pictures. To the doctor's horror, Margaret started to emerge shoulder first. The doctor had to push her back in to readjust her positioning before proceeding. Just after Margaret was delivered, Dave said, "Can you do it again? I don't think I got that shot." I could have killed him right then and there.

We arrived in the delivery room at 5:48AM. Margaret was born at 5:50AM. When Margaret was only a few hours old, my devoted husband whispered, "I am so glad you had this baby, now I can go to my high school reunion." Clearly, he wasn't vying for "Husband of the Year."

Margaret was born with jaundice and had to spend four days in an incubator. Due to the toll the delivery took on me, I was required to stay for observation as well. While I was recovering, Dave stayed home with Jessica and Sarah. I admit that I expected to come home to a dirty house, dirty dishes, and dirty children. When I arrived home with Margaret, I was pleasantly surprised to encounter just the opposite. The house was spotless, the children were clean, and even the laundry was done.

As we sat down for our first dinner as a family of five, Sarah revealed Dave's secret. "I liked it when Daddy was babysitting. He let us stay in the same clothes and we ate out of the pot!" Apparently, Mr. Not-Quite-Mom had cleaned and dressed the girls that morning for the first time since I'd been gone to create an illusion of perfection.

Then, true to his word, he left to attend his high school reunion in Ohio. He took Jessica and Sarah with him, leaving me alone with the baby. He said that he figured three young children would be too much to juggle in my weakened state. After they left, I immediately felt lonely. Almost daily, I would take Margaret to Marie Callendar's for lunch. I would invite strangers to sit and eat with me so I would have someone to talk with. Unintentionally, this resulted in a myriad of free meals.

When Margaret was two weeks old, we went for a check-up. The doctor insisted we get an X-Ray taken of her shoulder. Upon reviewing the X-Ray, he discovered that Margaret had broken her collarbone near the neck during delivery. For four months, she had to wear an orthopedic shirt that held her arm in place. Margaret hated that shirt and would cry whenever she saw it. Her pain and terror broke my heart.

Once I was home, I phoned my mother-in-law to let Dave know what was going on. He wasn't home so she assured me that she would relay the message. Unfortunately, when Dave got back to his mother's house, she mixed up the message and told him that Margaret had broken her neck. He was frantic when he called me back. I quickly set the record straight.

Dave returned home after being away for five weeks. Secretly, I loved that time alone to bond with Margaret, but I was happy to have my whole family in one place again.

# Aerodynamics

I have always been fascinated by the ability of children to find intrigue in everyday objects. Until, that is, my *own* children scatter that intrigue all over the floor. Two instances stand out in my mind.

The first one occurred when Margaret was a year old. I was in the kitchen washing dishes when I heard a bizarre combination of sounds. "Schuuu... Weeeee... Chucka Chucka Chucka..." I turned off the water and listened more closely. Again, I heard, "Schuuu... Weeeee... Chucka Chucka Chucka..." After a few seconds I realized that it was coming from the living room, so I headed in that direction. I heard the sounds again and, as I turned the corner, I immediately discovered the source. Margaret was sitting with my button tin on her lap. She was scooping the buttons up with both hands and throwing them into the air, causing it to rain buttons all over the room! Over the next few days, I did my best to retrieve the stray buttons, but I continued to stumble upon loose buttons until we moved six years later. I am still not sure if I ever *really* found them all.

The second instance involved my two oldest daughters. Jessica was around six years old and Sarah around 4 years old. Jessica had found what she thought was a foolproof way of creating a ruckus without taking any of the blame. She would convince Sarah to create mischief, even going as far as walking her through the process. Then she'd deny any responsibility for the act. After all, there would be no fingerprints or other proof that Jessica was involved, right? Well, Jessica tested this theory every opportunity she had. One day, I walked into the hall during one of Jessica's experimental tests of Sarah's gullibility, and I almost had a heart attack. Sarah had managed to procure the large bottle of talcum powder that I kept on the top shelf in the hall closet. Jessica was instructing her to jump up and down while squeezing it. When I asked, in shock, what they were doing, Sarah replied that they were "making snow." I admit it, the place looked like Aspen. Jessica quickly chimed in with her usual monologue, "It wasn't me. It wasn't me." But I knew that Sarah was too young to have acted alone. My biggest concern, at the time, was what the powder would do to their lungs if they inhaled any of it. I rushed them out of there and I spent the rest of the day rewashing the linens, dusting the area, and scrubbing the furniture. The vacuuming alone took over two hours.

Our children attempted other feats to try our patience and push the boundaries. The "fun things to do," which they invented throughout their childhood, grew more complex as they got older. However, those first endeavors were some of the messiest.

# A Christmas Story

On Christmas, in 1979, Dave and I thought it would be a great adventure to see how the holidays were celebrated in some other part of the world, like Europe or Australia or... Northern California since that's what we could afford.

We drove up to San Francisco on Christmas Eve. We arrived a few hours before midnight. We had just enough time to unpack before midnight masses would start. When we were leaving, we asked the person at the front desk where we could find the nearest church. It was relatively close by, so we decided to walk there.

The church was lovely, and the people were relatively friendly. Although, we did receive odd looks from several of the arriving parishioners. We weren't from the area, but we didn't let it deter us from attending the service. About halfway through the service, I started to realize that something was unusual about the congregation, but I couldn't put my finger on it. After shushing my sleep-deprived children for the 50th time, it finally dawned on me. My three little ones were the only little ones in the room. After I pondered that for a moment, it occurred to me that the congregation also seemed to lack heterosexual couples.

I wasn't bothered by this realization, but I believe the other parishioners were embarrassed for us. Particularly those sitting in our immediate vicinity. They were avoiding eye contact and fidgeting awkwardly. When it came time to share the peace, it appeared as though the congregation had decided to address the awkwardness by avoiding us and pretending none of it was happening.

Sarah, who was about four-and-a-half, was much bolder than I. She didn't concern herself with the possible consequences of a confrontation. She tried to greet the man in front of us, and he ignored her. This was foreign to her, and she must have assumed that he hadn't heard. Without hesitation, she picked up the prayer book and lobbied it at the back of the guy's head. It struck him so hard that I'm still surprised he didn't start to bleed. When he turned around, holding the spot where the book struck, Sarah stood as tall as she could and stuck out her little hand, proclaiming in her best big girl voice "PEACE OF DA LORD!" This man, clearly afraid of confronting Sarah's wrath again, shook her hand. I was utterly embarrassed. I wanted to leave, but I didn't want to create a scene. I was sure things couldn't get any worse.

When it came time to finish the service, the minister invited the congregation to join in a few "Christmas Carols." Before the choir could begin, Sarah started to belt out "Frosty the Snowman" at the top of her lungs. Jessica, who was old enough to know that "Frosty" was not what the minister had in mind, laughed at Sarah but sang along anyway. To our surprise, some members of the congregation chimed in as well. Sarah didn't stop there. After "Frosty the Snowman," she sang "Jingle Bells," "Rudolph the Red-Nosed

Reindeer," and a charming rendition of "Happy Birthday... Jesus." I was praying that the Lord would let me sink into the linoleum, but before it was over, the whole congregation was humoring her by singing along. As we left the church, the parishioners were more friendly, and the minister made it a point to greet us asking, "Now, who's our little choir mistress?"

Leave it to a child to remind us that we all originate from the same stock, and it is our own insecurities and reservations about what is different between us and other people, which build the barriers between us. If only we could learn to tear down those walls, the world might just be a better and more harmonious place to live.

# Oscar

Several months before Margaret was born, we adopted a new puppy. It wasn't something we had planned on doing but one of our neighbors was giving them away and I am my mother's daughter. Along with the pleadings of Jessica and Sarah, my heart bled for the little rascal.

This wasn't the first pet for our family, and, per our tradition, my daughters were asked to name the new addition. The girls were obsessed with *Sesame Street* at the time, so the mutt was christened "Oscar the Grouch." Unlike his namesake, Oscar was a friendly and sweet puppy. He was playful and generally well-behaved. Shortly after we took him in, Oscar started to grow... and grow... and grow. As he grew, we started to notice the strands of his mixed breeds: St. Bernard, Malamute, and German Shepard. Within a few months he was so large that if he stood up while under the kitchen table, he could lift the table off the ground! I was sure that he was a descendant of "Clifford, the Big Red Dog."

About a week before Margaret was born, I was getting increasingly worried that our dog wasn't going to be taken with the baby. The day I brought Margaret home from the hospital, I sat on the couch with her in my arms and watched as Oscar approached us. He sniffed her, then walked away and laid down in the middle of the living room floor. As he lay on the floor, he never took his eyes off Margaret and I was sure he was thinking, *what a strange new squeak toy.*

Around one o'clock the following morning, I got out of bed to check on Margaret. As I neared the nursery, I heard Margaret crying along with a low 'grrrrrrr' coming from inside the room. My heart started racing, I ran the rest of the way to the nursery, crashed through the door and flipped on the light switch. I froze when I saw Oscar cautiously raise himself off the floor and slowly approach me while he maintained a low growl. It was like he needed to know I had the proper clearance before I could enter. Once he was satisfied with my credentials, he started to bark fervently. He appeared outraged that I had taken so long to get to Margaret's side. I knew then that I didn't have to worry about Oscar hurting the baby. In fact, it was quite the opposite.

From that day on, Margaret could do no wrong in Oscar's eyes. We couldn't yell at her for anything, or Oscar would growl at us for the inappropriate treatment of "his baby." If we needed to punish her, Oscar had to be taken outside first. When this happened, we would hear Oscar ramming into the sliding glass door.

As Margaret grew, Oscar was her constant companion. She would use him as a bed, and he even taught her to walk. She'd grab onto the scruff of his neck; he'd stand and walk her across the room. As she hobbled around, she babbled that she was "walkin' da dog."

When Margaret was two years old, the unthinkable happened. Our neighbor gave his son a BB-gun for his birthday, and his son decided to use our house for shooting practice. The kid hopped the fence into our yard and proceeded to shoot out every single window within range. When he spotted Oscar, he started shooting at his feet. One of the BBs ricocheted off the cement and hit Oscar's side. When I came home with Margaret, I saw the broken windows and started panicking. I ran through the rooms to assess the damage and determine the cause. One of the most horrifying discoveries was how much glass had fallen into Margaret's crib. I cried at the thought of what might've happened had she been lying in there. When I reached the kitchen, I looked toward the backyard and spotted Oscar who, with a broken hip, had managed to corner his attacker so that he couldn't escape. "Good Dog," I screamed from my position as I dialed the police.

Thanks to Oscar, we didn't have to go to court to get compensated. It was obvious who was to blame. The neighbors agreed to pay for all the house repairs and Oscar's hip replacement surgery. If it weren't for Oscar, we might've been in the dark about what happened.

# My Fourth Child

I can say, with full confidence, that my daughters love their father and think of him as the "fun" parent. He was the one who played chase with them around the house, let them stay in the same clothes all day if I wasn't around, or took them out to play *Ms. Pac Man* on Friday nights when they were younger. I love that my girls have such a great relationship with their dad. However, Dave's lighthearted bond with the girls didn't always surface at the most appropriate times.

The worst examples of their poorly timed shenanigans are the ones that used to occur the moment we would cross the church threshold on Sundays. It was inevitable that, at some point during the service, one of them would make some little comment that would send the rest of them into fits of suppressed laughter that wouldn't end until after communion. It was at these times that I would gladly have disowned them all. I quickly discovered that to control my mini mob, I really needed to be three people. Then, I could have sat between each of my daughters *and* their father. I eventually became accustomed to this foolish behavior displayed by my family, since it had been surfacing almost every Sunday since Jessica was only a couple of years old. One day, when Margaret was a little girl, something happened that caused me to join in their little laughing games.

Margaret was still too little to appreciate the idea of "quiet time," so Dave and I had the challenge of finding a way to keep her from screaming out loud during Sunday mass. After a short while, Dave invented a game called *Bopping Heads.* The name of the game speaks for itself. Dave usually initiated their church-time playtime by lightly tapping Margaret's forehead with his own forehead. Margaret, in turn, would bop his forehead with her forehead and so on.

Margaret enjoyed this game immensely. You could often hear her little baby giggles all throughout the church whenever they played it, which was significantly better than little baby screams. Once, while the congregation was reciting the *Lord's Prayer,* my husband was sitting at the end of our pew with Margaret on his lap. In response to Dave's *bop,* my daughter leaned back as far as she could and slammed Dave's forehead so hard with her own that my husband fell backwards out of the pew. It was so unexpected that we all laughed. When he collected himself, I was relieved to discover that he hadn't suffered a concussion.

Sometimes Dave and the girls still act like hoodlums when it is highly inappropriate, but as they get older, they seem more aware of when it is suitable to be on one's best behavior. Yes, even Dave. After all, I believe he learned a lesson that day in church. *Never again play Bopping Heads with a two-year-old linebacker.*

# My Compliments to the Chef

Margaret went through her "I'm a big girl" phase when she was about four years old. Since Margaret is our youngest, this stepping-stone in her development nearly broke my heart. One night, when we were dining out, I realized just how fast my littlest girl was growing up.

Dave and I had decided to take our daughters to a nice sit-down restaurant. This was a breath of fresh air for us; a "gourmet dinner," with three girls under ten, usually consisted of a happy meal and a playground. As we sat there, my two oldest children perused the options on the kiddy menu, debating between the mac and cheese or hot dog and fries. Margaret wasn't at all interested in these choices. She put down the paper menu, looked at me, and asked, "Can I order from the big person's menu, please?" We tried to encourage our children's independence. Although we were skeptical, we agreed. We watched with suppressed smiles on our faces as Margaret's two tiny hands clutched onto a menu that was practically as tall as she was.

Margaret, not yet knowing how to read a menu, simply looked at the pictures to make her choice. After a few minutes she pointed to one of the pictures and asked, "What's that?"

"A Chef Salad," I replied.

She considered my answer. Then, after apparently deciding that she needed more information, she asked, "What's in a Chef Salad?"

"Well; egg, bacon, turkey, ham, cheese, lettuce, tomato..." I answered, pointing to the ingredients in the photo as I named them.

"Okay, I'll have that," she decided after a moment.

*Rrriight*, I thought.

To dissuade her, Dave told Margaret that, if she ordered the salad, she would be expected to eat every bite of it. After all, the Chef Salad was more expensive than either of our meals. Margaret nodded in understanding. When the waitress came to take our orders, Margaret stated with total seriousness, "I'll have a Chef Salad with blue cheese dressing on the side." The waitress looked at her with disbelief and then looked at us to see if we were going to object. I nodded to let her know that it was okay and the rest of us placed our orders.

When our dinners arrived, a salad was placed in front of Margaret that could easily have ended world hunger. Dave and I figured that we had lucked out. Despite Dave's insistence that Margaret had to finish her meal, he knew that after a few bites she would be full. Then, since we are such considerate parents, Dave and I would have shouldered the responsibility of polishing off her salad for her.

As the dinner continued, however, her salad continued to get smaller. About half an hour later, Margaret put the last fork-full into her mouth. She hadn't even shared one bite. From that day on, I assumed that Margaret must have a hollow leg. It's the only way to explain how that little child could pack away all that food without even breaking a sweat.

# Where Is

When Margaret was little, we use to play a game called "where is." The game was simple. Margaret would ask me where someone was, and I would tell her. One afternoon the game went like this...

Margaret: "Where is Jessica?"

Me: "Jessica is in class, probably studying arithmetic."

Margaret: "Where is Mommy?"

Me: "Mommy is sitting on the floor, sorting socks."

Margaret: "Where is Daddy?"

Me: "Daddy is on his way home from work."

Margaret: "No, *your* Daddy."

Me: "*My* Daddy is in Heaven."

Margaret: "Why?"

Me: "Because he got sick and died."

Margaret: "What's died?"

Me: "It's when you go to sleep and don't wake up."

Margaret: "Why'd he not wake up?"

Me: "Because he got sick."

Margaret: "Why?"

Me: "Because he didn't exercise, and he smoked too much."

At this point I began to cry. Then Margaret climbed up onto my lap and hugged me. As she gave me little finger pats, she said, "Oh it be ok. It be ok. But next time you see him, you tell him to be more careful."

# Photos 1970s to Present

*Our Wedding (June 24, 1972)*

*Happily Married! (1972)*

*Marine Corps Ball (1972)*
*'I dyed my wedding dress to save money'*

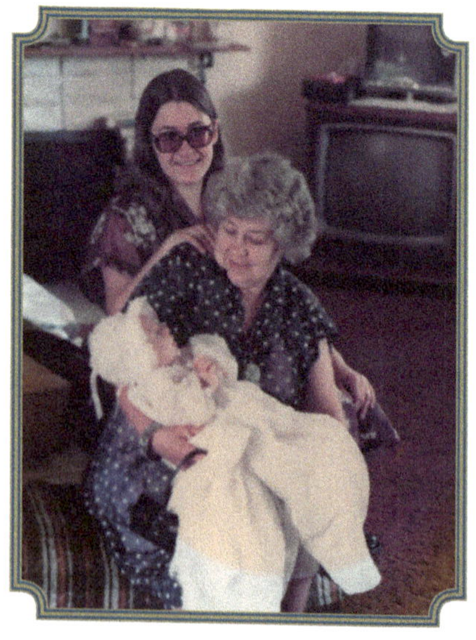

*Me, Mama, and Sarah*
*(Sarah's Christening 1975)*

*Dave and I with Jessica- 2 years old and Sarah- newborn (1975)*

*Jessica and Sarah (1977)*

*Dave with Margaret (1978)*

Margaret, Jessica, Sarah (front) with Santa (Christmas 1978)

Sarah, Margaret, Jessica (Disneyland 1979)

Me, Sarah, Jessica, Dave, Margaret (front) (1984)

*Last Photo taken of all the Sluppick children (1990)*
*Back Row: George Jr, Saro, Mike*
*Front Row: Frances, Juanita, Evelyn*

*Last Photo taken of the Jones Family (2015)*
*Left to Right: Sarah, Dave, Margaret, Evelyn, Jessica*

# Epilogue

I am the youngest of three, and in many ways, I am a lot like Mom, but like my sisters I am a complete Daddy's girl. I was Mom's last chance to have a "Mommy's girl" and for the first few years of my life it looked like it was going to happen. However, I will always remember her horror when I picked up a bottle of mustard and poured it all over my hotdog, proudly announcing that "I love mustard," a condiment Mom detested, and Dad loved. Even though we all ended up being Daddy's girls, there is one thing each of us inherited from Mom: our love of stories. We all love a good story, but it mostly revolves around actual books. The memoirs and Non-Fiction we devour are about historical events or famous people, not someone who raised us. None of us may have recognized it in childhood, but Mom was a born storyteller. I, unfortunately, often got bored hearing the same stories on repeat, and would often tune Mom out. Or worse, I would mockingly finish her stories as she was telling them.

At the age of 13, I discovered that my love for stories would be my future when I proudly announced that I planned to be an English major in college. It was then I started really investigating deeper meanings and symbolisms in the books I read. When I was around 15, I was listening to Mom tell one of her many stories, one I knew by heart at this point, but I found myself really listening for the first time. It was at this time that I revealed something to Mom about my young brain. Despite Mom being five years younger than Dad, as a young girl I always pictured Dad's childhood in bright technicolor and Mom's childhood in greyscale. Dad didn't sugar-coat his mischievous boyhood ways, and his stories were filled with underage shenanigans and all-around trouble making. While Mom's stories were filled with being a good and helpful child, who rarely got in trouble. Some of her stories did involve moments of her being mischievous, such as in "Playing House," but even then, the stories, in my young mind, were straight out of an old movie. Much of this had to do with Mom needing to grow up faster than most children after the loss of my grandfather. The truth is, it is often difficult for children to imagine their parents as children themselves, and we must rely on the stories we are told to form these images.

Even though it took me several years to really appreciate the stories Mom told, I was around seven years old when I discovered that she was an excellent storyteller. I will never forget the day I first hung onto every word my mother spoke. I was in second grade; my school was having career week, and both of my parents agreed to give presentations. It was amusing that I was thinking of this event, and then began re-reading "It's Magic," a story I hadn't read or thought about in several years. It was then I realized that Mom and I had something in common, an eye-opening revelation of a parent during Career Day.

During my career week, Dad was due to speak early in the week, and Mom was coming in toward the end of the week. As I already mentioned, I'm a "Daddy's Girl," and was excited for him to come talk about being a letter carrier. I expected him to wow my classmates and for them to see him as being the superman I knew he was. I bragged to everyone about how awesome Daddy was, and how everyone was going to love him. At the same time, I dreaded

Mom coming, because she wasn't as amazing as Dad, and so I barely talked about her upcoming visit.

The day Dad showed up for his presentation, he came out in full uniform with his mailbag and proceeded to bore my entire class to sleep. I was devastated. Where was the man who was funny, amazing, and lovable? He did, luckily, win back points when at the end of his presentation he said, "No letter carrier has an empty bag," and proceeded to pull out a couple bags of candy for the class. I didn't understand how the man who could do no wrong could be so incredibly dull. This made my dread for Mom's appearance heighten, because if my Superman could bore a class of 30 seven-year-olds, Mom was going to be so much worse.

The day of her appearance, I was scared that I was going to be labeled the "kid with the worse parents." In walks Mom, in her full nurse's uniform and holding a casserole dish covered completely in foil. She started with, "I am a Registered Nurse, and I care for people with traumatic brain injuries." She proceeds to talk about brain injuries and why it is important to protect our heads from injuries, and my entire class hung on to her every word. After a few minutes she asked the class, "Who knows how to ride a bike?" The entire class raised their hands. She then followed up with, "How many of you wear helmets when riding a bike?" The hands almost all went down. In the 1980s, while helmets were encouraged, they weren't required, so it was not uncommon for young children riding around the neighborhood without any protective gear. In my neighborhood, my sisters and I were the only ones to wear protective gear during any activity, and that day I understood why Mom forced me to be the "uncool" kid.

After the hands went down, she removed the covering off the casserole dish to reveal a huge Jello mold in the shape of a brain. She continued her presentation: "Imagine, you are riding your bike, and hit something, you get thrown from your bike, and your head hits the ground. Now you may feel a little headache, and on the outside, you look fine, but what about your brain?" She then proceeded to hit the side of the casserole dish, and the Jello mold started shaking violently, some pieces even breaking off as they hit the side of the dish. As the Jello continued wiggling violently in the dish, she continued talking about what might occur after this brain injury. As she wrapped things up, she pulled out some plastic bowls and asked, "Now who wants to eat some brain?" My entire class rushed to the front to get their fill of delicious fruit flavored brain.

I realized then that Mom knew how to captivate an audience, which is the first step to any great story. Her stories are what people remember most about her. When she passed away in 2016, at the reception every single person I spoke to inevitably talked about a story she had told them. Although, I used to get annoyed at hearing the same stories for the umpteenth time, Mom's ability to spin a tale is something I will always miss about her.

I want to thank everyone who has taken the time to read this book. When we lost Mom, I was grateful that Sarah and I began this journey while she was still with us, because it allowed me to hold on to a little piece of our family history. We lost momentum in this book for a few years, and I couldn't explain why. Maybe it was too difficult because of Mom's sudden passing or maybe it was simply that life got in the way. When Sarah approached me about finally finishing this book, I jumped at the chance, because I wanted the world to get to know the woman that I was proud to call Mom. During the final stages of putting this together, I found myself often tearing up, remembering all these stories, and thinking of all the ones we did not include. I could almost hear her voice again, and that has been my greatest gift in working on this book.

The group of stories you just read are a fraction of the stories Mom would tell us on repeat, and when I initially thought about compiling the stories into a book it was the title I presented to Sarah before any other ideas. Like so many other parents, my mom often got frustrated and would utter those three little words: "You never listen." While it is true that those were often words spoken after being told to clean our rooms or to take out the trash for the tenth time, I felt it was a fitting tribute, not just to Mom, but to all those parents out there who don't believe their children listen to them. Trust me, we do listen. We may not always listen when told to do our chores, but we listen to what's truly important.

*Margaret Rose Jones*

# Acknowledgments

Margaret and Sarah would like to thank their beta readers, Jessica Reeves and Emmanuel Hernandez; your feedback was critical in completing a more comprehensive set of stories. They would also like to thank their sensitivity readers, Kathryn Ervin and Bryan Hunt; your insight ensured we did not unintentionally portray harmful stereotypes or biases.

In addition, they'd like to thank John Mamaril for his advice on the publishing process, Veronica Scott for formatting and design, and Dr. Koolitz for the implanting of the idea.

Sarah would also like to thank her husband for his emotional support and patience, especially during the final months leading up to the publication.

Finally, they would like to thank their family members for filling in some lost details, especially their dad David, their sister Jessica, and their Aunt Juanita. And, most importantly, God, for blessing them with the mother that made all this possible and the strength and endurance to see this project through.

Margaret can be contacted via

- Email **shakespearefan78@hotmail.com**
- Instagram **@shakespearefan78**

Sarah can be contacted via

- Email **starintraining@hotmail.com**
- Instagram **@sarahladema**

# About the Authors

**Margaret Jones** grew up in Southern California, She earned several English degrees at CSU San Bernardino. She taught College Composition and Critical Thinking for over 10 years. She now works at DHL and lives in Kentucky with her dad and 3 cats.

**Sarah Jones-Hernandez** grew up in Southern California. She has degrees in Theatre for Acting and Dramatic Literature from California State University San Bernardino. She spent a year in the United Kingdom studying Shakespeare and directing a production of *The Reduced Shakespeare Company's: The Complete Works of William Shakespeare (abridged)* at the University of Hull. She currently works for the Walt Disney Company. She lives in West Covina, CA with her husband, Jose.